PICTORIAL HISTORY OF
SHIPS

PICTORIAL HISTORY OF
SHIPS

J H Martin

TREASURE PRESS

First published by Sundial Books Limited

This edition published by Treasure Press
59 Grosvenor Street
London W1

© 1976 Hennerwood Publications Limited
ISBN 0 907407 21 8
Printed in Hong Kong

Contents

The Age of Fighting Sail

ON 17 NOVEMBER 1665, when the English and Dutch were at each other's throats, Samuel Pepys went to bed later than usual. As Clerk of the Acts, one of the four principal officers of the Navy Board, he had been writing a long letter to the Duke of York, the Lord High Admiral, about 'the ill condition of the Navy' and its need of money 'before it be too late'. That need was already a familiar theme in English naval history.

Just over 60 years earlier King James I had inherited from Queen Elizabeth a maritime fighting force which was to set a standard in ship design for more than two centuries, until the coming of steam. The English believed in the 'round' ship. With its ability to face heavy weather and to carry stores for a long voyage, it had served them well, and under Sir John Hawkins they had learnt to reduce its limitations as a vessel of war. By increasing its length in proportion to its breadth, they made it less 'round' and clumsy. It also looked less top-heavy and was better rigged, with a larger and more effective sail area.

From the time that Henry VIII, Elizabeth's father, introduced the broadside, the Navy was no longer seen as merely a fleet of vessels carrying armed men in 'castles' fore and aft. The 'great guns' on their carriages revolutionized the structure of the ships, as well as their purpose and the warfare in which they engaged. Weapons so big and heavy obviously had to be placed below, on the main cargo-deck. When one of Henry's shipwrights took the alarming step of cutting holes in the sides for the guns to fire through, the navy of the future was born. If the first vessel to have gunports was indeed the *Mary Rose* (with the *Great Harry*, or *Henry Grâce à Dieu*, the second), we may some day look upon the pioneer herself, put together from the remains lying off Spithead.

In making the old lofty upperworks unnecessary, the guns removed much of the dangerous top-weight. The less exaggerated forecastles which remained were set well back from the stem, and the awkward stern constructions were replaced by a quarter-deck and poop (or half-deck, quarter-deck and poop), each of them shorter than the one below. All the ships had the square tuck, or transom stern.

These improvements were accompanied by changes in rig. In the fleet which met the Spanish Armada, ten of the largest vessels had four masts and nearly all the others three. The fourth mast, the bonaventure mizzen – the second or outer mizzen, stepped well aft – grew in favour until it was driven out by the use, from 1618, of square topsails on the mizzen-mast. With the discovery that sail power could be better obtained in this way, the shipwrights let the bonaventure mizzen disappear; by 1640 it had gone from the English Navy.

Between 1611 and 1618, in King James's reign, a sprit-sail topsail was added, on a mast at the forward end of the bowsprit, where it remained, despite the exposed position, as late as the middle of the eighteenth century. The early Stuart period also brought in the general use of topgallants, developed from Hawkins's idea of topmasts which could be easily struck and sent down to the deck. They were standard equipment for the larger men-of-war by 1600, but the smaller vessels were still without them; these craft, of which little is known, had a rig of six sails: spritsail, fore course, fore topsail, main course, main topsail and lateen mizzen.

Links with the past inevitably remained. The fleet which confronted the Armada was still, in composition, the 'Old Navy of England'. Of the 197 vessels under Howard and Drake only 34 were 'Queen's ships'; the others, all 163 of them, belonged to private persons. The Elizabethans had not broken away completely from the medieval conception of the Navy as an emergency force composed of any ships that could take fighting men to sea. We feel very close to feudal times when we learn that the *Revenge* carried longbows and sheaves of arrows, together with harquebuses and hackbuts fired from forked rests or laid over the bulwarks. (There were 1,540 soldiers among the 15,925 men who waited for the Armada; on the Spanish side more than half the total were soldiers – 18,973 out of 30,656.)

Let us consider the *Revenge* for a moment. That famous man-of-war, Drake's flagship in the fateful summer of 1588, earned a place in naval history at the time of her completion for John Hawkins's fleet eleven years before the Armada. Two shipwrights of superlative ability, Matthew Baker and Peter Pett, built her as a new kind of warship, a floating gun-platform. She has a strong claim to be called the first sailing ship-of-the-line.

She carried 34 guns: 22 demi-cannon, cannon-perriers, culverins and demi-culverins on a single gundeck, and a dozen sakers, long five-pounders. Demi-cannon threw a 32lb shot, cannon-perriers a 24lb, culverins an 18lb and demi-culverins a 9lb.

We find the *Revenge* described as a fast, handy vessel of 500 tons measuring 92ft along the keel with a beam of 32ft, and lying 'low and snug' in the water. Besides being well-gunned, she could stay at sea for long periods and was easy to manoeuvre in close action. She was a four-master, with topmasts that could be struck in accordance with the new method adopted by Hawkins and welcomed as 'a wonderful ease to great ships'.

Her normal complement was 250: 150 sailors, 24 gunners and 76 soldiers. The light for them was poor even in daytime. At night, when most of them slept on the bare boards of the gun-deck wrapped in blankets and coats, they had the help of the 'purser's dip', a candle in a horn lantern.

England was proud of the *Revenge* and proud too of all the ships which had defeated the Armada. When Elizabeth died in 1603 she left James a fleet containing no more than 29 vessels of 100 tons and over; but those 29 represented the nucleus of a Navy which had destroyed the ambitions of the most powerful monarch on earth. 'I protest before God and as my soul shall answer for it that there were never in any place in the world worthier ships than these are': the words are the Lord Admiral's but they might have been her own.

Her successor was determined on a friendly settlement with Spain. After the war had ended, the Navy fell into neglect while its affairs were administered by incompetent and dishonest officials. From the highest of motives, the peace-loving James put an end to the letters of marque sanctioning the private capture by merchant-men of enemy ships and merchandise 'as reprisals'. Thereafter corsairs and privateers became so daring round the shores of Britain that seamen could not leave port without the risk of spending the rest of their lives as galley slaves. Any merchant captain who retaliated

could be hanged from his own yardarm as a pirate. Landing at places in Cornwall, Devon and Ireland, 'Turks' from North Africa carried off young people to join the enslaved crews on the Barbary coast. Between 1609 and 1616 they captured nearly 500 English vessels. The 'Dun-kirkers' even levied a toll on ships using the Thames.

With the Narrow Seas full of terror, England's maritime trade declined appallingly. Seamen without employment at home went to work for the Dutch, and in the Medway noble ships rotted at their moorings, the Navy lacking the revenue from licensed privateering which had provided funds in Elizabeth's day. If Sir Walter Raleigh had written his projected treatise on sea power for Prince Henry, any part of it concerned with the Navy of his own time would have been melancholy indeed; but the Prince died, and in 1618 the King sent Raleigh to the block.

Opposite previous page: 'The Resolution in a Gale', by William van der Velde the younger.

Below: Henry VIII's Great Ship, the Henry Grâce à Dieu *or Great Harry. The four-master of 1,000 tons was begun at Erith on the Thames in 1514, rebuilt in 1540 and destroyed by fire at Woolwich in 1553. In May 1520, the King went aboard her at Dover on his way to France and the Field of the Cloth of Gold.*

Right: A London Science Museum 1:48 scale model of a galleon belonging to the late sixteenth century.

Among the few new men-of-war launched in James's reign was the *Prince Royal* of 1610, the largest ship which had yet been built. Some historians describe her as the first three-decker in the English Navy and others as the first two-decker: she had two full batteries and an armed upper deck. What first caught the eye was her decoration, the rich painting and gilding, the badges and coats of arms, the great carved lions' heads for the round gunports. The warships of Henry VIII and Elizabeth had been gaily coloured above their hulls, which were treated with a mixture of oil, turpentine and resin and left unpainted. Panels, arches and pillars, and geometrical designs were painted in bright contrasting colours on the upperworks. The *Revenge*, for instance, displayed the Tudor colours, green and white. Red was also favoured. On Elizabeth's ships yellow and purple, and occasionally blue, were seen. The sterns bore the Royal Arms, which may have been carved as well as painted, and there was an elaborately carved figurehead; but the *Prince Royal* introduced a completely new style. She looked so much a work of art that Phineas Pett who designed her was accused of making a showpiece rather than a man-of-war.

In 1637, working with his son Peter, he added the *Sovereign of the Seas* to the Navy of Charles I, who had succeeded James twelve years before. This historic three-decker, often referred to as the *Sovereign* or *Royal Sovereign*, was laid down at Woolwich on 16 January 1636 in the presence of the King and was launched in October of the following year. At the time of her building she displaced about 1,500 tons and was 232ft in length overall (with a keel of 127ft) and 46.5ft in beam, with a draught of 22.2ft.

She was a three-master, the bonaventure mizzen having vanished almost completely by that date. A well-known engraving by John Payne shows her with royals on the fore and main masts and a topgallant sail on the mizzen. These details, once questioned, are confirmed by a manuscript Navy list for 1640 at the Science Museum in London. Critics of the engraving – a copy of which Samuel Pepys hung in his green chamber – accepted that the 'Maintop Royal' and 'Foretop Royal' of the *Royal Sovereign* had been peculiar to that ship. At the end of the eighteenth century they came back into use as 'royals'.

Until the Restoration the *Sovereign* was the only English warship of 100 guns. In size and design the Navy's first true three-decker marked such an advance on any earlier vessel that she was hailed as 'this Britain's *Argo*', the eighth wonder of the world. To the ordinary person she was splendour afloat. Gerard Christmas, the royal master-carver, had ornamented her after drawings by Van Dyck, and at her prow a glittering equestrian figure, Edgar the Peaceful,

trampled on seven conquered kings. She cost in all £40,833, to which £24,753 was added for the guns: the £6,691 spent on the inside and outside joining and the painting and carving would have paid for a 40-gun ship complete.

To the Dutch 'the eighth wonder of the world' was the Golden, or Gilded, Devil. She took part in the St James's Day Battle of 1666, the year of the Great Fire of London, and she was also in action against the Dutch at the Kentish Knock (1652), Solebay (1672) and the Texel (1673). By the time of her last battles, Beachy Head in 1690 and Barfleur in 1692, she was no longer a devil to the Hollanders; they had become the allies of England against the French. In the end the enemy which destroyed her was fire: after 60 years she caught alight accidentally at Chatham.

She was the queen of the Ship Money Fleet, her construction and lavish embellishment paid for out of the hated levy which helped bring about the Civil War in England. The King's decision to revive the Elizabethan naval tax and extend it so that it included inland communities as well as seaports and coastal counties, was itself thoroughly sound. It offered England a permanent force at sea, maintained by the people, in place of the old ramshackle arrangement of a temporary fleet provided by the monarch. Ultimately the nation accepted it; but the person who made it acceptable was Oliver Cromwell.

Under him the home waters were cleared of pirates, the maritime trade improved dramatically, and the Navy entered a new era of efficiency and strength. Money was no longer spent on exuberant decoration: indeed at one time, before the rules were eased, the ships appeared in

puritan black. Among other changes, the height of the hull above water was reduced and the length of the keel increased. Vessels became steadier and more weatherly; but no big improvements were made to the sails and rigging, and the sail area remained small in relation to tonnage.

Under the Commonwealth, the seamen were given a fairer deal – prompt and correct pay (at first), better care ashore when they were sick or wounded, and more opportunities for advancement.

The Cromwellian zest for organization extended from the Articles of War, which became the basis of all subsequent naval law and discipline, to the sailors' food – two pounds of beef or pork daily (or one-and-a-half pounds of fish on certain days) and one-and-a-half pounds of bread (really biscuit) and a gallon of beer; and from the food to a code of tactics governing the ships in battle. Fighting Instructions set out the manner of attack, with an agreed use of gun-and-flag signals. To take full advantage of the broadsides, the ships fought in line-ahead formation, as ordained by Blake, Deane and Monk (later Duke of Albemarle) on 29 March 1653, four months before Monk defeated the Dutch off Scheveningen.

When the Civil War began in 1642, the Navy had 34 vessels of between 300 and 850 tons, as well as the *Sovereign* and *Prince*, handsome first-rates. In the eleven years of Cromwell's rule it acquired, under the Navy Commissioners who had replaced the Navy Board, no fewer than 207, of which 121 were still on the active list at the Restoration. By the end of 1651 more than 20 ships suitable for the line of battle had been added, and at the beginning of the First Dutch War in the spring of 1652 another ten were launched or on the stocks. Twenty-two new men-of-war entered the water in 1654 alone.

In May 1652 the Dutch could muster about 115 warships and the English 85; but Cromwell's vessels were superior in power. Eighteen of them mounted over 40 guns, whereas most of the Dutch had between 20 and 30. Tromp's flagship, the *Brederode*, stood out from all the rest with 59, the next most formidable carrying 48; the Hollanders possessed nothing to set against the *Sovereign*. Having to provide for the coastal waters and the river estuaries, their shipbuilders had evolved a man-of-war with a shallow draught and two gun-decks.

Off Portland Bill in 1653 Tromp lost twelve warships and 43 of the merchantmen which they had been convoying. Only one of Blake's ships, the 32-gun *Sansom*, was sunk. The Dutch also lost about 5,500 men killed, wounded or taken prisoner compared with 1,200 on the English side.

Ironically, the Parliamentarians left Charles II an impressive fleet of 154 vessels when he took over in 1660. As a further irony, Charles introduced the title 'Royal Navy' although the finance was still raised on the Cromwellian system of national taxation. He returned to England from Holland in the *Naseby*, renamed the *Royal Charles*. Three years later a jubilant crowd burnt her figurehead, which depicted Cromwell on horseback trampling on six nations. To replace it with a carving of Neptune cost Charles £100.

The King could ill afford to spend money on a figurehead or a new coat of arms (preserved at the Rijksmuseum in Amsterdam) for the stern. Parliament had fallen into debt; despite its good intentions, the seamen were owed nearly

£400,000 just before the Restoration; some of them had not been paid for three or four years. With a fine Navy, the King also inherited a large debt. Shipbuilding declined and the old abuses came back.

Fortunately for England, the King, in reviving the Navy Board, appointed Samuel Pepys as Clerk. At the age of 27 Pepys entered upon his duties with intelligence and vigour. Through the administration which he set up as Clerk of the Acts and later as Secretary to the Lord High Admiral, this highly capable young man, son of a tailor and a washmaid, and at the same time a kinsman of Lord Sandwich, made himself, in Sir Arthur Bryant's words, the 'saviour of the Navy'.

Pepys's great difficulty was the old one of cash. From the diary that he wrote we learn of his distress at the 'lamentable moan of the poor seamen that be starving in the streets'. Naval service was not continuous: in peacetime the sailor was paid off, to find other work, or to beg, until the next emergency. When it occurred, there was no overwhelming rush of volunteers. Needing men in large numbers, the press gangs descended on coastal towns and villages, grabbing recruits left and right. Merchant seamen, tailors, ploughboys, men with the palsy, lads who could speak only Welsh – they were all the same to the 'press'. Some had never seen a ship before.

At sea the men lived between the guns. Kegs and sea chests formed their seats; any shelves or cupboards which they fixed in place had to be jettisoned when battle was imminent. On shore, free for a while from the stench, the unspeakable food on a long voyage, the iron discipline with its terrifying punishments (a third of the 39 Articles of War carried the death penalty), they

made happily for the taverns.

Again and again such men as these saved England. One of the Royal Navy's great advantages in the wars with the Dutch was its superior morale. We can detect the sheer zest of the English sailors in the journals kept by Edward Barlow, the Prestwick farmhand's son who had never seen a ship until he walked from Manchester to London and was puzzled by the strange objects floating in the Thames. His vessels included the *Naseby* (or *Royal Charles*), the *Augustine*, one of the men-of-war sent against the Barbary pirates at Algiers, the frigate *Monck* and the *Royal Sovereign*.

The *Monck* served in the Battle of St James's Day in the Second Dutch War, which began in March 1665 after an expedition sent to America by the King's brother, the Duke of York (later James II), had captured New Amsterdam, which immediately became New York City, together with New Netherland. At the beginning of hostilities the English had about 160 ships, 5,000 guns and 25,000 men to oppose about

Far left: Hendrik Cornelisz Vroom's oil painting of the 56-gun Prince Royal at Flushing. She was built by Phineas Pett and launched by King James I in 1610. Under the Commonwealth she was renamed the Resolution. She surrendered to the Dutch in 1666. Note the Prince of Wales's plume of feathers.

Near left: A drawing by Van der Velde the Elder of the ornamentation on the stern of the Royal Charles. In the Second Dutch War she was the flagship of the Duke of York. Admiral Sir William Penn, whose Quaker son founded Pennsylvania, was Great Captain Commander. The Dutch towed her off during their raid on the Medway.

135 ships and a slightly smaller number of guns and sailors than their own. The Duke of York commanded the battle fleet as Lord High Admiral.

In June of the following year, after a Dutch victory in the Four Days' Fight and an English victory in the St James's Day fight which followed it, de Ruyter dealt his enemies a shattering humiliation by sailing up the Medway, past all the alleged defences and obstacles, raiding Sheppey, destroying the fort at Sheerness, and burning and sinking the 70-gun *Royal James*, the 90-gun *Loyal London* and the 76-gun *Royal Oak*. Many smaller vessels were also sunk, blocking the channel. To crown this breath-

Above: 'The True Portraicture of His Ma.ties Royall Ship The Soveraigne of the Seas.'

taking impudence, the Dutch carried off the *Royal Charles*. Her carved and gilded stern may be seen in Amsterdam today.

The Dutch Wars brought a higher degree of order into sea fighting. Fleets had grown so large and unwieldy that they were arranged in three divisions, each of them under an admiral flying a distinguishing flag; the Admiral of the Fleet a red flag in the centre, the Vice-Admiral a white flag in the van, and the Rear-Admiral, commanding the rear squadron, a blue flag. It was eventually realized that vessels in the line of battle should not be mixed, the weak with the strong. The powerful became the true 'ships of the line'; the rest were allotted other duties. All were rated according to the number of guns they carried.

Above: John Paul Jones, commanding the Bonhomme Richard, *attacks the* Serapis, *a frigate of 44 guns, off Flamborough Head in Yorkshire on 23 September 1779. The duel was one of the fiercest naval actions in history. Early in 1976 plans were announced for an international attempt at raising the* Bonhomme Richard *which went down with her unconquered flag flying.*

Right: The Shannon *and the* Chesapeake *in desperate combat off Cape Anne, near Boston, on 1 June 1813. The* Shannon *was the victor.*

Much of our knowledge of Restoration warships derives from the drawings and paintings of the Van de Veldes, the father and son who left their home in Holland and served as marine artists to Charles II. They are known to have set up their easels in the Queen's House at Greenwich, now the central part of the National Maritime Museum, which has 1,450 of their pictures. Anyone studying the Royal Navy of that period should visit Greenwich and also the great Rijksmuseum in the Dutch capital. The Van de Veldes saw the ships of war in action.

Another source of information is the Pepys Library at Magdalene College, Cambridge. The collection left by Mr Secretary Pepys includes Sir Anthony Deane's *Doctrine of Naval Architecture*, which contains a series of draughts and a set of masts and rigging plans for each of the six rates composing the fleet. From the draughts and the Van de Velde drawings we are able to see that since Elizabethan times the sterns have

become rounded.

For knowledge of the later Stuart vessels we depend largely on the scale models built, as a new practice, when the ships were laid down. There were no great changes in design. Projecting galleries built along each quarter in Elizabeth's reign, primarily as latrines for the officers (the men used a deck of gratings – the 'heads' – at the fore end), were embellished and later covered in completely (the *Sovereign* provides an example). In the *Royal Prince* of 1610 they were carried round the stern, to form a stern-gallery, or stern-walk, a fashion which then died out for some 80 years.

The most important change in rig was the introduction of staysails and jibs. By 1690 studding sails, said to have been invented by Raleigh in Armada year, were regularly employed. In a Van de Velde picture of the Battle of Solebay a line of reef points – short ropes for securing the sail when it had been reefed – can be seen across the upper part of the main and fore topsails. The men-of-war at the end of the century had much the same rig as their successors at Trafalgar.

In building the *Royal James* Anthony Deane experimented with the use of iron standards (upright posts between decks) and knees (angle pieces). We do not know if the idea was successful; the *Royal James*, flagship of the Earl of Sandwich, was set ablaze by a fireship at the Battle of Southwold Bay a year after her launching. Iron standards and knees solved a problem after the Napoleonic Wars when good bent timber was hard to find.

Deane also tried out a new form of sheathing, employing milled lead instead of wood to hold in place the layer of tar, hair, sulphur and tallow covering the underwater part of the hull. It served for about ten years before it was abandoned because of the corrosion caused by electrolytic action with iron and lead together in sea water. A better process, brought in after the Restoration, was studding: the use of broad-headed nails hammered close together over the bottom and covered with a mixture of tallow and resin. Corrosion again occurred when a frigate was given a full set of copper plates underwater in 1758.

Eight years after Deane had made his name with the *Rupert* and the *Resolution*, both laid down at Harwich, he went to Portsmouth as Commissioner and built the *Harwich*, one of the fastest vessels in the fleet and the forerunner of ten others like her. She had been copied from the 70-gun *Superbe* which visited the Thames with other French ships in 1673. The English were beginning to take a great interest in French men-of-war. Shipwrights across the Channel had discovered science: the proportions of a hull, the forces acting upon a mast – these and other subjects relating to naval architecture were

studied by French mathematicians, and theory was put into practice.

No one knew how much interest the French and their warships would soon command. In the winter of 1688 a fleet set out from the Scheldt bound for England: William of Orange was on his way to claim the throne of his father-in-law. He landed safely at Brixham in Devon while James's ships, which had assembled at Thames-mouth, were held back by ill winds. After escaping unhindered to France, James reached Ireland with French support, was defeated at the Battle of the Boyne, and embarked for France again. England and Holland, the two great Protestant maritime nations, now found themselves united against Louis XIV. The curtain was rising on a bloody drama that would continue, with intermissions, until 1815.

In 1690, the year of the Boyne, England had 100 ships of the line in a total of 173, and her ally 69 in a total of 102. Against these the French could muster 221 vessels, of which 93 were ships of the line. It was the age of great admirals. For generations to come men would speak with pride of Benbow off Jamaica directing the attack with his right leg shattered; of Hawke at Quiberon Bay, throwing formal tactics to the winds, and of Old Dreadnought Boscawen off Lagos; of Rodney at the Saints, off Dominica; of Howe and 'the Glorious First of June', the famous victory in 1794; of Jervis off Cape St Vincent, where Nelson in the 74-gun *Captain* left the hallowed line and fought the Spaniards for a short time alone.

Yet the English ships were inferior to the French. The vessels of the enemy had longer keels, finer underwater lines, a better proportion of length to breadth, deep holds, longer gun-decks, and lower-tier gunports far enough above the water for the guns to be employed in rough weather when the corresponding ports in the English vessels had to be closed. The English men-of-war pitched, tossed and heeled alarmingly, emphasizing the lowness of the ports. They also lacked sound timbers, largely because suitable oak was increasingly hard to obtain, and they were over-gunned. In the dockyards conservative rule-of-thumb methods fitted

Pages 16 and 17: 'The Constitution *and* Guerrière *dropping Astern' by Thomas Birch. Before the* Guerrière *sank, Americans and British worked together transferring the wounded to the* Constitution – *which is afloat at Boston today.*

comfortably into a background of sloth and ignorance, fraud and neglect. A long-overdue visitation ordered by Admiral George Anson in 1749 was not repeated for another 20 years.

In the course of making improvements, Anson clarified the rating of ships by laying down that those fit to stand in the line were first-rates, three-deckers of 100 guns or more; second-rates, three-deckers of 90 guns; and third-rates, two-deckers of 74 or 64. The others were 'cruisers': the fourth-rates, two-deckers of 50 guns (occasionally 60); the fifth-rates, frigates of 36 guns; and the sixth-rates, frigates carrying from 28 to 32. At the middle of the eighteenth century the 74-gun ship became the standard medium class of third-rate, and the frigate – a word which had been given at least half a dozen meanings – acquired firm definition as the 'eyes of the fleet', a fast cruiser for scouting and raiding, with its guns on a single flush deck.

Improvements continued throughout the eighteenth century. During the first decade the steering wheel superseded the whipstaff – a vertical lever pivoted to the deck and able to

were yellow, crossed by black spars. Blue could be seen here and there, particularly on the stern-works, and scarlet was employed for relief. The painters liked to be as generous as they could with gilt. All in all, the vessels were brighter, better ventilated, healthier and more seaworthy than they had ever been before.

Well before 1800, a new navy came into existence on the other side of the Atlantic. Ships had taken the first English colonists to the New World, ships maintained their links with the home country, and craft of various kinds handled a good deal of the transport within America itself. The Thirteen Colonies could therefore call upon their own maritime resources when the trouble with the Crown grew acute.

Early in 1775 the Continental Congress bought and armed two merchant ships of about 450 tons, the *Black Prince*, renamed the *Alfred*, and the *Sally*, renamed the *Columbus*. It also obtained six brigs or brigantines, three schooners and five sloops, to which Washington's army added four schooners in Massachusetts and a sloop and two schooners on Lake Champlain.

throw the tiller sideways, though not far. We can sum up the progress in sail power by describing the man-of-war at the end of the period as a full-rigged ship.

About 1720 the hulls were light brown or deep cream in colour, an improvement on the nondescript tarry look produced by earlier economies. In the second half of the period they were coated with black or yellow, as the captains preferred. The familiar pattern of black divided into bands by yellow along the sides of the gun-decks, with the black port-lids on the yellow creating a chequerboard effect, was generally adopted in the 1790s. Ochre (a cheap colour) replaced the dark red of the gun-decks themselves. Masts

In these craft the Continental Navy had its beginnings.

At the end of 1775 the Congress ordered thirteen brand-new vessels, to be built by the following spring: the *Hancock, Raleigh, Randolph, Warren* and *Washington*, of 32 guns; the *Congress, Effingham, Providence, Trumbell* and *Virginia*, of 28; and the *Boston, Delaware* and *Montgomery*, of 24. Four were laid down at Philadelphia, two each at Newburyport, Poughkeepsie and Providence, Rhode Island, and one each at Baltimore, Chatham in Connecticut and Portsmouth in New Hampshire.

A private yard had launched a fourth-rate, the *Falkland*, in 1690, and some other men-of-war

had followed her – enough to establish a tradition of naval shipbuilding. It also helped the colonists that their shipwrights were especially skilled at constructing fast, cheap vessels, craft which could be employed against pirates, smugglers and others who gave trouble, besides serving the ordinary needs of small communities. For half a century before the Revolution the fast schooner was so much in evidence that the New Englanders believed they had invented it, at Gloucester, Massachusetts, in 1713.

With the coming of war the Americans were able to design and build some of the finest men-of-war afloat. Other ships were obtained from abroad. The *Bonhomme Richard* lost in battle

with HMS *Serapis* off Flamborough Head, Yorkshire, was an old French East Indiaman, the *Duc de Duras*, renamed in honour of *Poor Richard's Almanac* and its originator, the astonishing Benjamin Franklin who was mainly responsible for bringing France into the war on the side of the colonists.

Important to the general course of events was the Battle of Chesapeake Bay, or the Virginian Capes, fought on 5 September 1781 between the British fleet ('British' since the Union of England and Scotland in May 1707), under Rear-Admiral Thomas Graves, and two combined French fleets, with 36 ships of the line, under the Comte de Grasse. Victory went to the French and the

American Revolution was saved. 'It was the Battle of Chesapeake Bay', declared Sir Geoffrey Callender, the maritime historian, 'which decided the final issue of the war.'

After the Revolution the Americans disposed of their army and navy and for a time were without any defence forces apart from the local militia companies. Meanwhile they built up a large merchant marine. Their ships traded across the oceans, and when they were preyed upon in the Mediterranean by Barbary corsairs the President and Congress authorized, in March 1794, the construction of six frigates. Three of them were 44s: the *United States* laid down at Philadelphia, the *Constitution* at Boston

and the *President* at New York. Although the other three – the *Constellation* at Baltimore, the *Congress* at Portsmouth, New Hampshire and the *Chesapeake* at Gosport, the naval yard at Norfolk, Virginia – were supposed to be 36s, the War Office re-rated them as 38s before they had been completed.

Early in 1797, the year when the *Constitution*, *Constellation* and *United States* were launched, Sir John Jervis with fifteen ships of the line attacked a Spanish fleet twice as strong in size and fire power and won a victory which assured the British that if the French tried to invade their shores they would not have any naval help from the government at Madrid. During the battle,

Above: The Battle of Trafalgar. 'Now, gentlemen, let us do something today that the world may talk of hereafter,' said Collingwood off Cape Trafalgar. Many years later Alfred Thayer Mahan, the American naval historian wrote: 'It was those far-distant storm-beaten ships, upon which the Grand Army never looked, which stood between it and the dominion of the world.'

off Cape St Vincent 100 miles south east of Trafalgar, Horatio Nelson sailed his two-decker, *Captain*, across the path of the *Santísima Trinidad*, the flagship of Juan de Cordova and the biggest war vessel afloat. After engaging her, he attacked the *San Josef* of 112 guns and the *San Nicolas* of 80.

Greater glory lay ahead for the sailor from Norfolk. In 1798 he became a national hero with his victory at the Nile. Jervis had defeated the Spaniards at Cape St Vincent, Adam Duncan had destroyed the Dutch at Camperdown, a few miles off their coast, and now Napoleon's army in the Egyptian desert was cut off from home through the ruin of its fleet. So hard fought was the battle that when, towards midnight, the fighting slackened, men fell asleep in utter exhaustion beside their guns. About two hours earlier, the flagship *Orient* had blown up. The British did not lose a single ship.

Seven years later, when the Royal Navy consisted of 88 ships of the line, 125 frigates and about 140,000 seamen, the victor of the Nile went into battle again with the French, this time off Cape Trafalgar. His flagship, HMS *Victory*, a three-decker of 100 guns and 2,162 tons burden, was already 40 years old, if allowance is made for 'middling repairs' between 1783 and 1792 and a rebuilding between 1800 and 1803. She measured 151ft along the keel, 186ft along the gun-deck, and 226ft overall, with a beam of 52ft, and she set 31 sails, not including the studding or steering sails used when the wind was light. Her main topsail was 60ft on each side, 55ft along the head and 90ft along the foot. The mainmast, with topsail and topgallant, rose 175ft above her deck, and the main yard was 110ft long. Her guns needed a range of less than half a mile to be really effective, and at close quarters they could pierce five feet of solid oak – with the round shot brought to white heat if any attempt was being made to set the enemy ship on fire.

The first-rate had a complement of 633. Those on board her a few days before Trafalgar, at the last muster, included one African, 22 Americans, one Bengali, two Danes, seven Dutchmen, three Frenchmen, four Italians, two North Germans from Hamburg, one seaman from Madras, four Maltese, three Norwegians, two Portuguese, one Prussian, one Russian, six Swedes, two Swiss and nine from the West Indies.

Nelson had decided to attack the Franco-Spanish force, which was stronger than his own, at two separate points. While he bore slowly down upon the enemy line supported by the *Téméraire* and *Neptune*, both of 98 guns, Collingwood led the southern column in the *Royal Sovereign* with the *Belleisle* astern. In the silence, the tense windless hush, the *Victory* made a signal which would be remembered when all the details of the fighting were forgotten: 253 269 863 261 471 958 220 370 4 21 19 24 – 'England

Expects That Every Man Will Do His Duty'. (There was nothing in the code book for 'duty' and so it had to be spelt out: 4, 21, 19, 24.) By the end of that day the Emperor Napoleon, though still ten years from final defeat, had no chance of invading Britain unless he built himself another fleet.

Nelson had admired the American naval force in the Mediterranean. 'There is in the handling of those transatlantic ships', he said, 'a nucleus of trouble for the Navy of Great Britain.' He was right. Seven years after his victory and death at Trafalgar the young United States boldly took up arms over Britain's claim to have the right of searching neutral ships for deserters. Inevitably, with the ocean between, the war itself had a strong naval character. The Americans were known to possess only a small navy, seven frigates and eight sloops; but three of the frigates, the *Constitution*, *President* and *United States*, were in fact ships of the line called the 'pocket battleships'.

The War of 1812 produced several American naval heroes and some famous sea-fights – above all the duel between the *Constitution* and the *Guerrière*, off Cape Race on 19 August in the first year of hostilities (for the War of 1812 lasted until the end of 1814). After the *Guerrière* had been turned into a blazing hulk, the British accepted defeat, and victors and vanquished joined in helping the wounded. On 30 August the *Constitution* entered Boston in triumph, to report the first surrender of a British captain in a single ship action since 1803, two years before Trafalgar. The American victory made Captain Samuel Hull a national hero and gave a great boost to morale, especially in New England where opinion had been strongly opposed to 'Mr Madison's War'.

While the British were still shocked by the news of 'HM late ship *Guerrière*', further American successes added to their dismay. On 25 October 1812 Captain John Carden of HMS *Macedonian* offered his sword in surrender to Captain Stephen Decatur of the *United States* after an engagement in which one hundred of his men were lost, more than a third of all on board. Only then did he learn about the *Constitution* and the *Guerrière* and discover that he was not, as he had supposed, the first Briton to haul down his colours to an American.

On the first day of June the following year, the American frigate *Chesapeake* under James Lawrence lost her brief and furious battle with the *Shannon* off Cape Anne. For Americans the defeat was eased by the conduct of the wounded Lawrence. His own refusal to admit defeat – 'We have met the enemy and they are ours' – gained him the final victory of the war after two British ships, *Detroit* and *Queen Charlotte*, collided while he was defending Detroit at the western end of Lake Erie.

The age of fighting sail did not end with the war of 1812. British warships were improved by two Surveyors of the Navy. Between 1813 and 1832 Sir Robert Seppings introduced a complete system of diagonal framing, together with round sterns and bows; and then Captain William Symonds, his successor, concentrated on making the vessels faster. He gave them well-rounded midship sections and finer underwater bodies, and completely closed in the opening at the waist to create a continuous upper deck.

In 1827, a fleet of British, French and Russian ships went into battle against a Turkish force in the Bay of Navarino where the Athenians had forced the Spartans to surrender in 425 BC. It was the last battle fought under sail, and a very important one in that it secured the independence of Greece. While the British lost 75 killed, the

Previous page: HMS Victory was ordered on 14 July 1759, laid down at Chatham on 23 July 1759 and named on 28 October 1760. She was launched on 7 July 1765. She has been preserved at Portsmouth since 12 January 1922.

French 43 and the Russians 59, the Turks were estimated to have had over 1,000 killed and 3,000 wounded.

Preserved sailing warships can still be seen today. At Portsmouth, almost one hundred years after the Battle of Navarino, Nelson's flagship *Victory* was being restored to its original condition. At about the same time, USS *Constitution*, also known as 'Old Ironsides', was similarly preserved in Boston, Massachusetts, with the help of public subscription.

As long as some of the old battleships endure, they will remind us of the age of fighting sail, of the men-of-war Turner painted, of the vessels which inspired Ruskin to say:

Take it all in all, a Ship of the Line is the most honourable thing that man, as a gregarious animal, has ever produced. By himself, un-helped, he can do better things than ships of the line; he can make poems and pictures, and other such concentrations of what is best in him. But as a being living in flocks, and hammering out, with alternate strokes and mutual agreement, what is necessary for him in those flocks, to get or produce, the ship of the line is his first work. Into that he has put as much of his human patience, common sense, forethought, experimental philosophy, self-control, habits of order and obedience, thoroughly wrought handwork, defiance of brute elements, careless courage, careful patriotism, and calm expectation of the judgment of God, as can well be put into a space of 300 feet long by 80 broad. And I am thankful to have lived in an age when I could see this thing so done.

Below: John Clevely, Senior, a shipwright at Deptford on the Thames, painted this picture about 1750. It shows the launch of a 74-gun ship at Deptford yard. The larger ship is probably the Culloden, *of 74 guns, launched there in 1747, and the smaller, still on the stocks, the* Rochester *of 50 guns, launched in 1749.*

The Triumph of Steam

ON 14 OCTOBER 1788 young Robert Burns went for a trip in a steamboat. The vessel consisted of two hulls with a couple of paddle wheels in line between them. In one part was the boiler and in the other the engine, which had two vertical open-topped Newcomen cylinders of four in. diameter by about eighteen in. stroke. Chain gearing took the power to the paddle wheels which drove the craft at the rate of five miles an hour. Those on board with Robert Burns were William Symington, who had designed the engine, Patrick Miller who had commissioned Symington to design one, James Taylor, who had recommended the use of a steam engine in the first place and Alexander Nasmyth, inventor of the steam hammer. In the words of James Taylor, the steamboat 'answered Mr Miller's expectation fully and afforded great pleasure to the spectators present'. The engine still exists, preserved at the Science Museum in London.

Thirteen years after that experimental trip on Dalswinton Lake, near Dumfries, William Symington produced an engine for the *Charlotte Dundas*, a 56ft craft built of wood. The engine, which had a single horizontal cylinder, drove a paddle wheel housed in a recess at the stern. As governor of the Firth and Clyde Canal Company, Lord Dundas thought that steam tugs might be used instead of horses to tow vessels along the waterway. The *Charlotte Dundas*, when she was tried out in March 1802, gave an excellent performance, steaming confidently against a strong wind which held up all the other traffic; but fears that the wash from her paddle would damage the banks led to her rejection.

The next important person to be impressed by a steamboat was none other than Napoleon. Working together in France, the Americans Robert Fulton and Robert R. Livingston had leased a steam engine of eight horsepower from the inventor, and had fitted it in a hull 70ft long with paddle wheels 12ft diameter. Fulton informed Napoleon of his plans, and the Emperor was attracted by the picture of invasion barges towed by steam tugs on a windless day when the British fleet could not stir.

However, the steamboat broke and sank under the weight of the machinery. Fulton raised her, working himself ill, and rebuilt her completely. 'During the past two or three months,' said the *Journal des Débats* on 9 August 1803, 'there has been seen at the end of the Quai Chaillot a boat of strange appearance, equipped with two large wheels mounted on an axle like a cart, while behind these wheels was a kind of large stove with a pipe as if some sort of fire engine were intended to operate the wheels of the boat.' At six o'clock in the evening the vessel began towing two other craft. For an hour and a half the spectators witnessed 'the strange spectacle of a boat moved by wheels like a cart, these wheels being provided with paddles or flat plates and being moved by a fire engine'.

The *Journal* continued: 'As we followed it along the quay, the speed against the current of the Seine seemed to be about that of a rapid pedestrian, that is, about 2,400 toises an hour [2.9 miles]; while going down stream it was more rapid.' Fulton was disappointed, having expected about sixteen miles an hour, and so was Napoleon. Clearly, Fulton's steamboat could not cross the English Channel, with or without an invasion fleet.

Back home in 1807 the inventor completed a steamboat at Paulus Hook on the Hudson. Before the vessel had moved, the local boatmen reacted violently, fearing that their livelihood was threatened, and Fulton had to post a guard at his workshop. The new vessel was 133 feet in length and thirteen feet in breadth, with a displacement of 100 tons. Her two paddle wheels, placed at the sides, were fifteen feet in diameter and carried radial floats four feet long and two feet wide.

On 17 August 1807 the *American Citizen*

reported briefly:

Mr Fulton's ingenious steamboat, invented with a view to the navigation of the Mississippi from New Orleans upward, sails today from North River, near State's Prison, to Albany. The velocity of the steamboat is calculated at four miles an hour. It is said it will make a progress of two against the current of the Mississippi, and if so it will certainly be a very valuable acquisition to the commerce of our western states.

Fulton called his vessel *The Steamboat*, advertised her as *The North River Steamboat*, applied to register her as *The North River Steamboat of Clermont*, and wrote of her as *The North River Steamboat* or *The North River*. The world remembers her as the *Clermont*, the first commercially successful steam vessel in the world. After attaining a speed of 4.7 mph on her trial run, she ran as a packet between New York and Albany until the end of the season. During the winter she was rebuilt and refitted.

By 1810 three Fulton steamboats were

operating, *Clermont* and *Car of Neptune* on the Hudson service and the *Raritan* on the route to New Brunswick. In all he produced 20 successful craft, including the warship *Demologos*. He died before he completed the *Empress of Russia*.

America had developed the steamboat so successfully that Europeans came to observe and report. One of the visitors was Jean Baptiste Maréstier. His report, read before the Institute of France, was published in 1824 by the Royal Press at Paris.

Maréstier told his fellow countrymen that the *Clermont* had made a trip to Albany, '120 nautical miles from New York', in 32 hours and had returned in 30.

At that time there was some uncertainty over the distances on the western rivers. Maréstier says:

No part of the globe offers opportunities for inland navigation to the extent that America does. Immense lakes, large bays, deep rivers, split the vast country in every direction. From the capital of Canada to that of the United States or even that of Virginia one can travel nearly 900 miles in eight days, making more than five-sixths of the trip in steamboats.

For years after William Symington's experiment in Scotland the world outside America remained strangely indifferent to the new mode of travel. Jonathan Hulls had been granted a patent for a steam tugboat in 1736; Jacques Périer had moved a small craft by steampower in 1775; the Marquis Claude de Jouffroy d'Abbans had run a steamboat successfully on the Saône in 1783; and in America there were notable contributions to steamboat progress before the end of the century. Yet in Britain nothing important was achieved until 1812 when Henry Bell from

Linlithgow, who had a hotel at Helensburgh, ran his *Comet* on the Clyde. It was 51ft in length overall and 11.25ft in breadth (15ft over the paddle boxes). The engine was fitted on the port side with a single upright cylinder placed above the crankshaft, which carried a balanced flywheel six feet in diameter. On the starboard side a low-pressure boiler set in brickwork provided the steam for turning two sets of radial paddles on each side – later replaced by a single pair of paddle wheels.

She was launched on 24 July 1812, and on her trials in August she steamed from Greenock to Glasgow, about 20 miles, in three and a half hours. Bell promptly advertised her for public service between Glasgow, Greenock and Helensburgh.

In 1816, the *Comet* was operating on the Firth of Forth and in 1819 she provided a steam link between Glasgow and the West Highlands. On 15 December 1820 she ran ashore after leaving Fort William. The first steamer to run commercially in Europe finished as a total wreck at Craignish Point.

Early one morning in the summer of 1819 lookouts at the flag-telegraph station on Cape Clear at the south-west corner of Ireland saw a vessel belching smoke and obviously on fire. They quickly gave the alarm to a naval squadron in the Cove of Cork and the revenue cutter *Kite*, with Lieutenant John Bowie in command, hurried to her aid. She was travelling fast and gave no sign of altering speed. Nor did she wish to be helped; on the contrary she fired several warning shots. Bowie and his crew were amazed by this behaviour, and also by the ship herself; she was running, they saw, under bare poles. They had no means of knowing that a steamship,

Opposite page 27: The old and the new.

Above left: Robert Burns was a passenger in Patrick Miller's first steamboat. The 25ft vessel was launched on 14 October 1788 with an engine built by William Symington, a mechanic born at Leadhills, Lanarkshire, in 1763. Travelling at 5 mph on Dalswinton Lake, near Dumfries, the craft 'answered Mr Miller's expectation fully and afforded great pleasure to the spectators present.'

Above: William Symington's Charlotte Dundas on her trials in 1802.

Opposite: 'When Sail Beat Steam.' From Frank H. Mason's painting of an incident in 1895: the Turahina outpaced the steamer Ruapehu in the Roaring Forties.

Above: Loading cotton on the Mississippi, from a Currier and Ives print.

Left: Henry Bell's Comet *of 1812, the first steamboat to run commercially in Europe. It had an engine built by John Robertson of Glasgow. After she had steamed about 20 miles from Greenock to Glasgow in 3½ hours, Bell advertised her for trips on the Clyde between Glasgow, Greenock and Helensburgh.*

after 7 pm, without the assistance of a single sheet, in a style which displayed the power and advantage of the application of steam to vessels of the largest size, being of 350 tons burden. She is called the *Savannah*, and sailed from Savannah the 26th of May and arrived in the Channel five days since; during her passage, she worked the engine 18 days. Her model is beautiful, and the accommodation for passengers elegant and complete; this is the first ship on [*sic*] this construction that has undertaken a voyage across the Atlantic.

After her Liverpool triumph, she visited Stockholm, where Charles XIV of Sweden wanted to buy her, and Petersburg, where the Czar Alexander I invited Moses Rogers to remain in Russian seas with his steamer. But Captain Rogers put out for home. The Elegant Steam Ship voyaged from the Neva to the Potomac by way of Copenhagen, Arendal, the North Sea, the Western Isles of Scotland and the Newfoundland Banks. She had rough weather. Reporting her arrival at Savannah in December 1819 the *Daily National Intelligencer* added: 'Her machinery has met with no accident; her wheels are so constructed as to be taken all on board in from ten to twenty minutes, which leaves the vessel in the same situation as any other ordinary ship, and as capable of resisting the action of the waves.'

She was admired for her looks and praised for her performance; yet her career as a steamship had already ended. In August 1820 she was auctioned. Her engine was removed, and in October she sailed with a full cargo and about 24 passengers, more than her total for the whole of her six months as a steamship. She served as a regular packet between New York and Savannah until she was wrecked on a sand bar opposite Fire Place, Long Island, on 5 November 1821.

Hardly anyone was keen to cross the Atlantic in a ship driven mysteriously by fire and steam. Shorter voyages were less alarming. In 1814 the 70-ton *Margery*, another steamship built on the Clyde, travelled down the east coast to London and opened a service on the Thames between Wapping Old Stairs and Gravesend. Two years later she crossed the English Channel. In 1818 a regular service began from Greenock to Belfast. Steam links were established in 1821 on three more routes, between Holyhead and Dublin, Dover and Calais, and London and Leith. The Leith run opened in March with the two-masted *City of Edinburgh* built for the General Steam Navigation Company, which was to become the oldest shipping concern in the world. She carried square topsails on her foremast. To press and public in 1821 her engines of about 100 horsepower were 'extremely powerful'. The future William IV and Queen Adelaide went on board her and expressed surprise at the magnificence of her passenger accommodation.

the *Savannah*, was on her way across the Atlantic from the Southern port of that name.

According to Moses Rogers, her sailing master, the crew of the *Kite* were permitted to come on board and examine the machinery, a courtesy which they deserved. Their mistake had been completely natural. Never before in history had a steamship crossed the Atlantic.

The guests returned to their cutter and the *Savannah* made for Liverpool, paddle wheels turning. Frank O. Braynard in his detailed history of 'The Elegant Steam Ship' (published by the University of Georgia Press) tells us that at 5 pm on the Sunday smoke began to rise from her bent stack. Her paddle wheels were assembled and all sails furled.

Among the arrivals yesterday at this port [says a press account] we were particularly gratified and astonished by the novel sight of a fine steam ship, which came round at half

In 1822 Wigram and Green launched the 180-ton paddle steamer *King of the Netherlands* for General Steam Navigation. While the Thames yard eagerly seized the new opportunities, building three steamers in 1823, the Clyde laid down the three-masted *James Watt*, which had a paddle wheel on either side and a thin funnel about as tall as her mainmast.

Continental nations had also begun to use steamers. In 1815 the Russian barge *Elizabeth* was given steam propulsion for service on the Neva, and in 1816 the *Prinzessin Charlotte* was ready to trail her smoke along the Elbe and Spree. These were river vessels using their engines as auxiliaries. Steam accepted, and passed, a more rigorous test in 1821 when the *Rising Star* left Gravesend on the Thames for Valparaiso. No record was made of the days on which she used steam.

Her paddle machinery was built by Maudslay, Sons and Field of Lambeth. In 1825 this company provided the engines for another pioneer, the 470-ton *Enterprise* built at Deptford and fitted out for a voyage to Calcutta after the Government of India had offered a prize of 20,000 rupees to any British company which established permanent steamship communication with Calcutta by the end of 1826. As the conditions required the vessel to arrive in not more than 70 days and the *Enterprise* took 113, she did not qualify for the award. But she received

half of it and was bought by the Indian Government. On her passage of 13,700 miles from Falmouth she used steam for 64 days.

In the year after this vessel and the smaller *Falcon* of 176 tons had completed the Calcutta passage, the Dutch Navy bought its first steamship, the 438-ton *Curaçao*, launched as the *Calpe*. The American and Colonial Steam Navigation Company of London had intended her to trade between Britain, the United States and the West Indies. Instead, under Dutch ownership and command, she left Hellevoetsluis, near Rotterdam, on 26 April 1827 with 57 persons on board for Paramaribo, the chief port of Surinam, where she anchored on 24 May, having travelled 4,000 sea miles in 28 days at six knots. Crossing again in the following March with 68 on board, she reduced her time to 25 days, for the first thirteen of which she kept up continuous steam power.

It was Maudslays who engined the 813-ton *Rhadamanthus*, an armed paddle steamer described as 'beautiful to look at, and as sharp in the bow as the bill of a snipe'. She was built by the Admiralty, the first steam vessel to be laid down at Devonport. In 1834 she travelled to Jamaica and back, using steam intermittently; her paddle-wheel floats were removed and replaced as needed.

The progress of steam navigation in the early nineteenth century is well illustrated by the

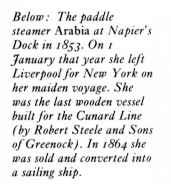

Below: The paddle steamer Arabia *at Napier's Dock in 1853. On 1 January that year she left Liverpool for New York on her maiden voyage. She was the last wooden vessel built for the Cunard Line (by Robert Steele and Sons of Greenock). In 1864 she was sold and converted into a sailing ship.*

career of the 206-ton *William Fawcett*. She was built for use as a Mersey ferry boat. After running on the Belfast, Dublin and London service of the Dublin and London Steam Packet Company, she was bought by the Peninsular Steam Navigation Company. The *William Fawcett* was run weekly between Falmouth, Lisbon and Gibraltar. The route was extended to Alexandria in 1840 and later to India, China, Japan and Australia, passengers and goods travelling from Alexandria to the Nile by the Mahmoudieh Canal and thence by steam to Cairo and through the desert as far as Suez, with the use of 3,000 camels for each shipload. The company was now the Peninsular and Oriental – the P & O, which today commands the biggest merchant fleet afloat.

Canadians had shown an interest in steam navigation ever since John Molson had opened a passenger service at Montreal in 1809 with the 85-ton *Accommodation*, a smaller version of the *Clermont*, and the first steamer built in Canada. On 18 August 1833 the schooner-rigged *Royal William* of 1,370 tons put out from Pictou harbour in Nova Scotia with seven passengers and 324 tons of coal. She was looking for new owners. After making three round trips for the Quebec and Halifax Steam Navigation Company, she had been quarantined during a cholera epidemic. The company suffered such a bad financial loss that it decided to dispose of her in England. She ran into a gale off Newfoundland, continued for ten days on the port engine alone, and reached Cowes in the Isle of Wight in seventeen days from Pictou. The full voyage from Quebec to Gravesend took 39 days. She is said to have used steam most of the time, with intervals for clearing the boilers of salt, a task which occupied about 24 hours every fourth day.

On 16 May 1840 the 648-ton steamer *Unicorn* left on a voyage in the opposite direction, from England to Canada. The Cunard Line acquired her in 1840 and sent her out to run between Quebec, Pictou and Halifax, linking with the service provided by the *Britannia* and her three sister ships. With 27 passengers on board, she put out from Liverpool on 16 May 1840, about three weeks before the *Britannia* left on her first crossing, and arrived at Halifax on the 30th, after fourteen days of wild weather. She then went to Boston where she received a great welcome. Her side-lever engines performed well. In November 1843 she rescued the survivors of the sail transport *Premier*, wrecked at the mouth of the St Lawrence. Three years afterwards she was sold and sent to California. She worked in the Panama and San Francisco trade until 1853 and then made her valiant way to Australia.

In all this time no vessel had crossed the Atlantic under continuous steam power. According to Dr Dionysius Lardner, professor of natural philosophy and astronomy at University College, London, such a voyage was 'purely chimerical'. Dr Lardner proved beyond all question that the ship would need more coal than she could possibly carry. One might as well talk of making a voyage to the Moon.

The learned doctor was lecturing on this theme to the British Association at Bristol in August 1836 when Isambard Kingdom Brunel politely challenged him from the audience. Brunel did not succeed in winning over the others present. But he was already on the way to converting them by an argument more powerful than theory. When someone at an early meeting of the Great Western Railway directors had wondered if the proposed line from London to Bristol was too

Left: In 1824 the Enterprise *made the voyage from Britain to Calcutta in 100 days, for 64 of which she used steam. Another account reports that she travelled to Calcutta via the Cape of Good Hope in 1825, steaming for 103 days out of 113.*

Below: Robert Fulton's Clermont *of 1807, the first steamboat to be a commercial success, was propelled on the Hudson by an engine from Boulton, Watt and Company of England. She ran on the river for seven years.*

long, he had answered, as the engineer: 'Why not make it longer, and have a steamboat go from Bristol to New York and call it the *Great Western*?' On 19 July 1837 the steamboat floated out of Patterson's dock at Bristol, and on 18 August she departed under sail for London, to be fitted with Maudslay engines. Crowds on the riverside at Blackwall gazed with astonishment at a ship of 'magnificent proportions and stupendous machinery'. She was a paddle steamer of 1,320 tons, 236ft in length and 35ft in the beam (58ft over the paddle boxes).

While the nation marvelled at her size, Brunel's rivals in London and Liverpool prepared to beat

Below: 'View up river from entrance to Old Dock, Bristol' by T. L. S. Rowbotham.

Bottom: Isambard Kingdom Brunel's Great Britain *returns home to Bristol in the summer of 1970. The ship was towed the 7,600 miles from the Falklands where she had remained since 1886.*

Right: Launching of the Great Britain *at Bristol on 19 July 1843. The Prince Consort performed the ceremony.*

the *Great Western* with two new vessels of their own. When it became clear that neither ship would be ready in time, the British and American Steam Navigation Company of London chartered the 703-ton *Sirius* of Cork in place of the *British Queen* and the Transatlantic Steamship Company found a substitute for the *Liverpool* in the 617-ton *Royal William of Dublin*.

After returning to Bristol, the *Great Western* left the mouth of the Avon for New York on 8 April 1838. One of her passengers, a young American, kept a detailed journal of the voyage. He writes:

As we neared the city, the first object to which our attention was now given was the *Sirius*, lying at anchor in North River, gay with flowing streamers, and literally crammed with spectators, her decks, her paddle-boxes,

Above left: The Admella, *once known as the fastest passenger steamship on the Melbourne–Adelaide run. She was wrecked in 1859.*

Below left: HMS Terrible *of 1845. Like the American paddle-wheel frigates* Mississippi *and* Missouri *in the same period, she contributed to the decline of the sailing warship.*

Previous pages: The William Fawcett, *a little over 200 tons, was built of wood by Caleb Smith of Liverpool in 1829 for use as a Mersey ferry-boat. The Peninsular Steam Navigation Company – later the P & O – opened its contract mail service from London to Lisbon and Gibraltar with this ship.*

her rigging, masthead high. . . . It was an exciting moment – a moment of triumph! Experiment then ceased – certainty was attained. . . .

Slipping down the Thames on 28 March, the *Sirius*, with the figurehead of a white hound carrying the Dog Star between its front paws, had dared the open sea and strong headwinds. Thanks to the determination and seamanship of her commander, Lieutenant Richard Roberts RN, she had won by a few hours the distinction of being the first vessel to cross the Atlantic entirely under steam. But she had nearly failed. She came in with only fifteen tons of coal left after sacrificing four barrels of resin from the cargo. The *Great Western*, on the other hand, still had 200 tons of coal in her bunkers, and she had also taken a day less to arrive. Together the two ships, big and small, had announced the triumph of steam. Brunel was to build two more historic ships, the *Great Britain*, which proved too big for her dock, and the *Great Eastern*, which was launched into the Thames sideways with immense effort and at the cost of about £1,000 for every foot won. But the *Great Western*, predecessor of the *Great Britain* by six years, refuted for ever the arguments of Professor Dionysius Lardner.

Not long before her arrival at New York, the two boilers of a Cincinnati paddle steamer had blown up, killing nearly all her 150 passengers and crew. But this disaster did not affect the welcome given to the ocean steamships or the increasing use which was being made of steam power on the inland waterways of North America. The steamboats had already earned a place in the history of the United States. As time passed, their white wooden filigree work, their chandeliers and pictures and gilded acorn decorations, created the style known to us as Steamboat Gothic. Nor have they entirely gone. Long after

Mark Twain wrote *Life on the Mississippi* from his experiences as a steamboat pilot, nostalgia is satisfied by the spectacle of stern-wheelers racing each other, as in a Currier and Ives print.

As time passed, the marine engine was greatly improved. Shipowners were offered an alternative to the reciprocating engine from the day in 1897 when Sir Charles Parsons' *Turbinia* startled the Navy at Queen Victoria's Diamond Jubilee Review. Four years earlier an alternative to steam itself had been patented by Rudolf Diesel, who disappeared mysteriously in 1913 after boarding a ship for England at Antwerp. The next revolution was the use of atomic power. But the nuclear reactor does not represent the complete break with the past that might be assumed. The heat which it produces is used to generate the same force that drove the *Clermont* and the *Comet*.

Below: Brunel's Great Eastern, *built of iron at Millwall. She was launched sideways into the Thames, after great difficulties, on 31 January 1858. For thirty years she was the largest ship afloat. Besides paddle wheels she had a screw propeller.*

Modern Warships

NELSON WAS AWARE of steam power. The ships which he commanded seem closer to the age of Drake than to the Industrial Revolution, so remote do they look from anything suggestive of boilers, cylinders, pistons and condensers. It may therefore surprise us to realize that a steam engine, Thomas Newcomen's, had worked successfully more than half a century before Nelson was born. Nelson showed an interest in the *Charlotte Dundas,* of Chapter II, yet nearly 20 years passed before the Royal Navy had its first steam craft, the 212-ton *Monkey,* a tug built at Rotherhithe on the Thames with an 80 horse-power engine. In 1882 the Admiralty added the paddle steamer *Comet,* launched at Deptford; she displaced 238 tons, was propelled at four to five knots by an engine of 80 horsepower and carried four nine-pounder guns.

Britain was mistress of the seas. So long as the Navy remained as it was, all would be well: any radical alteration – and nothing could be more radical than the abandonment of sail – carried the risk that it might be a change for the worse; and it was sure to be vastly expensive. Their lordships of the Admiralty had no wish to desert the old familiar ways in favour of strange and dangerous paths, mysterious to themselves and to the Service. They had a good deal of clear fact to support them. Before we condemn them outright as obstinate diehards, we must understand that the steam power which they saw at work was the steam power of that time, a heavy and cumbrous assembly of boilers, engines and paddle wheels. Boilers had a tendency to blow up and engines a tendency to break down – a failure that in battle could be calamitous – while paddle wheels had the double disadvantage of preventing the ship from firing a proper broadside and at the same time offering the enemy a hard-to-miss target. If the power unit had been far less awkward for a ship at sea, the paddle wheels would still have been a huge drawback. The unit itself, vertical and well above the waterline, was equally

vulnerable. 'Mr Speaker,' Lord Napier told Parliament, 'when we enter His Majesty's naval service and face the chances of war, we go prepared to be hacked to pieces by cutlasses, to be riddled with bullets, or to be blown to bits by shell and shot; but, Mr Speaker, we do not go prepared to be boiled alive'.

For the Royal Navy steam power continued to mean a few little tugs useful for towing sailing vessels in and out of harbour. No great change was made until the introduction of the screw propeller, pioneered in its adopted form by John Ericsson, a retired Swedish naval officer, and Francis Pettit Smith, an English farmer. The screw, unlike the paddle wheel, was completely out of the way, with the engines well down inside the hull. It seemed the perfect solution to a difficulty which had appeared insurmountable; but the Admiralty still held back. When Ericsson built a steam launch with twin screws, and towed Admiralty officials along the Thames in a barge at fully ten knots, their lordships raised the objection that a vessel could not be accurately steered when its driving force was at the stern.

Fortunately for Ericsson, the trial had impressed two Americans, Francis B. Ogden – an engineer who had been the United States Consul at Liverpool – and Captain Robert Field Stockton, an influential naval officer. Stockton enticed Ericsson to America.

The United States were ahead of Britain in the adoption of steam naval vessels. In 1814 Adam and Noah Browne of New York built the first steam warship, Robert Fulton's *Demologos*. She was an extraordinary craft, with two hulls joined at bow and stern. Between the hulls, and protected by them, was a paddle wheel. Besides carrying a battery of 32-pounders intended to fire red-hot shot from behind wooden walls five feet thick, she had submarine guns which could shoot 100-pound projectiles from below the waterline. A great hose from a steam pump was to play on the enemy decks, washing off

Opposite previous page: USS Bainbridge, *the nuclear-powered guided missile frigate.*

Above: The Great Britain *seen from another steamship.*

sailors and drenching the guns so that they could not be used.

Fulton built the *Demologos*, or *Fulton the First*, for the defence of New York in the War of 1812, but hostilities ended before she was ready, and her engine (of 120 nominal horsepower) had still not been installed when he died in February 1815; her guns sounded for his funeral.

The first screw warship was also American, the ten-gun sloop *Princeton*, built at the Philadelphia Navy Yard under the supervision of Robert Stockton and launched in 1843 as a vessel displacing 954 tons, with a deck length of 164ft and a beam of 30.5ft. Her 400-hp engine by Merrick and Towne of Philadelphia could

drive her at thirteen knots, owing to the use of a six-bladed screw of the Ericsson pattern. She was to mount twelve carronades and two twelve-inch wrought-iron guns, one designed by Ericsson and the other by Stockton. When the two were tried out on the quarterdeck, Stockton's burst and killed several people, among them the Secretary of State, the Secretary of the Navy and two Congressmen.

The first British steam warship was the 428-ton *Rising Star*, a wooden paddle ship constructed to the order of Thomas Cochrane, liberator of several nations and a champion of steam in the Royal Navy. In a picture of 1821 she is shown with two funnels and three masts. She was

steamer, the 60-hp *Diana* of the East India Company, launched at Kidderpore in 1823 for service on the Hooghli River. During the First Burma War (1824–5) Captain Frederick Marryat – not yet the author of *Mr Midshipman Easy* and *Peter Simple* – employed her to lead 63 ships and 9,000 troops upriver after the British capture of Rangoon.

Pettit Smith's screw proved its worth in a series of experiments conducted by the Navy in the steam sloop *Rattler* after Brunel's *Great Britain* had been given screw propulsion. To the great excitement of the Royal Navy and the shipbuilding world, the *Rattler*, a screwship, raced the *Alecto*, a naval paddle sloop of equal horsepower. She beat her opponent three times over – the third time by 40 minutes, on a 60-mile course dead into wind and sea. When the friends of HMS *Alecto* maintained that their favourite was nevertheless the better ship for towing duties, the Navy secured the two together, stern to stern, with a pair of cables, and called for full steam ahead as soon as the cables had tautened. After an interval in which neither ship seemed to

intended to go into battle against the Spanish in Chile, but by the time of her arrival at Valparaiso in April 1822 the Chilean revolution was over. For the remainder of her career, until she was wrecked in 1830, she ran as a privately-owned vessel; but she has a place in naval history as the first steam-propelled British warship to be launched (on 5 February 1821), as the first steamer to make a westerly crossing of the Atlantic – however much she may have depended on her sails – and as the first steamer to range the Pacific.

The one distinction which she missed, the Chilean revolt against Spain having already succeeded, came the way of another paddle

move, the *Alecto* was towed backwards, her paddles thrashing to no effect, at a speed of about two knots.

Convinced at last, the Admiralty ordered the frigate *Amphion*, then on the stocks, to be fitted with a screw. She was not launched until 1846. In that year the *Rifleman*, the first screw ship built in dry dock at Portsmouth, was taken to the Thames for her engines to be installed. Even then the Navy regarded the wind as the normal and desirable form of power. The captain liked to know that when he had a chance to use his sails he could order the screw to be lifted clean out of the water.

The first British ship of the line to have screw

Above: Guns at Jutland. At 5 pm on 30 May 1916, the British Admiralty partly decoded a German signal suggesting that an important naval operation was about to begin. Before midnight Britain's Grand Fleet was at sea, heading eastwards. In the morning the British and German warships steamed towards each other; and at 3.45 pm, off Denmark, the Battle of Jutland began.

machinery from the outset was the 91-gun *Agamemnon* of 1852, Admiral Sir Edward Lyons' 'superb *Agamemnon*' who distinguished herself at the bombardment of Sebastopol in the Crimean War. She was, in effect, a steam-powered sailing ship.

The first Royal Naval vessel designed to fight under full steam seems to have been the screw ship *Dauntless* of 1844. The *Arrogant*, laid down at the same time, had only auxiliary engines.

Although the *Dauntless* was propelled by a 580-hp engine, she proved slower than many paddle vessels. Screw machinery could not work at its best in a ship which had a wooden hull and a bluff stern; as John Scott Russell told a meeting of fellow naval architects in 1864, 'bits of wood kept together with bits of metal cannot stand the continuous day-after-day wear and tear of the wriggle of a 1,000-horsepower screw in the tail of a ship'.

Richard Trevithick and Robert Dickenson had taken out a patent for iron-ship construction as early as 1809, and in 1822 Sir Charles Napier had sponsored the paddle steamer *Aaron Manby*, which had a hull constructed of iron plates a quarter of an inch thick, with a wood lining 'to prevent heat being communicated to the cargo'. The Admiralty showed little or no interest in so

revolutionary a craft; but in 1840 it acquired a small iron packet ship, the *Dover*, and three years later it invited a number of shipbuilders to submit plans for 'iron vessels capable of carrying heavy armaments'. John Laird laid down the frigate *Vulcan*, soon afterwards named the *Birkenhead* after the Mersey port where she was built. In all, eleven shipyards went to work on a programme embracing no fewer than 33 iron vessels, of which about half a dozen were fighting ships and the rest auxiliaries.

Not long before, in 1840, the 170ft *Nemesis*, one of four gunboats built by Laird for the East India Company, had advertised the value of iron

(and also of watertight bulkheads) by remaining intact when she ran aground off the Scillies, and then, in the First Opium War, by repelling everything fired at her by the Chinese, who called her the Devil Ship and offered a reward of $50,000 for her capture. Resolutely unimpressed, the enemies of floating iron replied that the accident in the Scillies had occurred because the compass of the *Nemesis* had been affected by the metal. To them an iron ship was almost as much of a monster as the *Nemesis* had been to the Chinese. They insisted that enemy shot would easily penetrate the thin metal, shattering itself and the target alike and causing deadly splinters; that a hole in metal could not be repaired, unlike a hole in timber, by ordinary members of the crew, using simple tools, anywhere in the world; and that an iron vessel which had been holed

Left: The paddle sloop Alecto. *She lost her famous tug-of-war with the screw-driven* Rattler *in May 1845.*

Above: HMS Falcon, *one of the six fast torpedo-boats built on the Clyde by Fairfield from 1896 to 1900. She was sunk in a collision in 1918.*

Below: La Gloire *of 1859, from a painting by Le Breton.*

badly would go straight to the bottom instead of lying for a time on the surface, or floating half-submerged.

At Portsmouth in 1845 HMS *Excellent* fired for two days on the *Ruby*, a small iron steamer, and reduced her to scrap worth £20. The test was not a fair one, but it persuaded Sir Robert Peel, the Prime Minister, to desist from the folly of building iron frigates. Sir Charles Napier, having deserted his old cause of steam, warned the House of Commons that if the *Birkenhead* were unfit to fight she was also unfit to carry troops (the duty which took her to her terrible end off the foot of South Africa in 1852).

Eventually the French took the lead by constructing *La Gloire*, a wooden three-master of 5,600 tons displacement which had been given a belt of iron 4¾ inches thick along both sides.

Above: HMS Colossus, *the first dreadnought built on the Clyde. As Rear-Admiral E.F.A. Gaunt's flagship at Jutland, she sank a destroyer at 7.05 pm and opened fire on the leading German battle-cruiser at 7.12 pm before she was hit, without serious damage, at 7.16 pm.*

Below: Launch of the Fulton the First, *or* Demologos, *at New York on 29 October 1814. She was the first steam warship in history. Robert Fulton intended her for service in the War of 1812.*

Britain's answer to Napoleon III and Dupuy de Lôme, his *directeur de matériel*, was the famous *Warrior*, laid down at Blackwall in the summer of 1859. Her lines paid tribute to the graceful clippers pioneered in the United States, but she was twice as long as a contemporary clipper (420ft overall; 380ft 2in. between perpendiculars) and between her fore and main masts she had two telescopic funnels. For about five-eights of her length she was protected by wrought-iron plates 4½ inches thick bolted to an eighteen-inch teak backing. She displaced 9,210 tons. On her trials she made over fourteen knots, a speed not achieved by any other warship afloat.

Her gunnery lieutenant, the Jacky Fisher who one day would give his name to a naval era, wrote of her that 'it certainly was not appreciated then that this, our first armour-clad ship of war, would cause a fundamental change in what had been in vogue for something like a thousand years'. The historic vessel ended her seagoing career in 1884, became part of the *Vernon* torpedo school in 1900, and in 1923 was sold, to serve as an oil pontoon at Pembroke Dock in South Wales where she was visited by the Duke of Edinburgh just before he founded the Maritime Trust.

By the middle of the nineteenth century even the most passionate defender of Britain's wooden walls saw that they could not withstand the assault of the cylindrical shells fired by the new rifled guns which were being developed. Any remaining doubts were swept away when news

came of the duel between the Confederate iron-clad *Merrimac* (more correctly *Merrimack*) and the Federal ironclad *Monitor* in Hampton Roads, Virginia, and of the havoc wrought by the *Merrimac*, or *Virginia*, before she met her adversary. The navies of the world noted with great interest that the Confederate vessel had sunk the wooden sloop *Cumberland* by using her ram – after ignoring the *Cumberland*'s desperate broadsides – and that the Federal craft, designed by Ericsson, had consisted of very little more than a heavily-armoured revolving turret holding two eleven-inch Dahlgren guns (someone called her 'a cheesebox on a raft').

Rams soon appeared on warships new and old. One of them sank the *Re d'Italia* at the Battle of Lissa, between the Austrian and Italian fleets, off the Dalmatian coast. The Royal Navy proved the effectiveness of this primitive weapon all too dramatically on two occasions: in 1875 when HMS *Iron Duke* accidentally sank her sister ship the *Vanguard* during a fog in the Irish Channel, and in 1893 when HMS *Victoria* went down, with the loss of 359 men, after she had been rammed by HMS *Camperdown* owing to an error of judgment by Admiral Sir George Tryon, who perished with his flagship.

A year after the Hampton Roads battle of 1862 the French, Russian, Italian, Prussian, Brazilian and Peruvian navies were all turning to turret ships. Laird built two of them, *El Toussan* and *El Mounassir*, not for the Pasha of Egypt but – like the raider *Alabama* – for the Southern States. The Admiralty took them over when they raised the Confederate flag, and thereafter they were the *Scorpion* and *Wivern*.

The next historic man-of-war was Edward Reed's *Devastation*, completed at Portsmouth in 1873. She had two 35-ton muzzle-loaders in a forward turret and two more in a turret aft. Both constructions were turned by steam power. Everything else was relatively crude, but the *Devastation*, a steam-propelled iron vessel displacing 9,330 tons, marked such a break with the past that she can be regarded as the first modern battleship. Certainly she was the first to look like one: she had two funnels and no sails. The plating on her turrets varied in thickness from twelve to fourteen inches.

At this period a new weapon was demanding attention from the naval constructors. In October 1864 Lieutenant William B. Cushing, a superbly courageous officer of the United States Navy, had destroyed the Confederate ironclad *Albemarle* with an outrigger torpedo, a case of gunpowder held out on a spar over the bows of his vessel and touched off at the right moment by a line running to a detonator. But the torpedo of the

Below: HMS Fearless, *one of the light-cruisers at Jutland. For a period she was dazzle-painted in black, white, pink and pale green. She was sold in 1921, eight years after her completion at Pembroke Dock.*

1880s was an altogether different weapon, fired at its target from a distance. In time it created three new vessels, the torpedo boat, the torpedo-boat destroyer and the submarine – which Rear-Admiral A. K. Wilson, V.C., the Controller of the Navy, dubbed a 'damned un-English weapon' when the Admiralty, in 1900, ordered five American Hollands to be laid down under licence by Vickers at Barrow-in-Furness, Lancashire. John Philip Holland, an Irish American, was a leading pioneer of the submarine a century after Robert Fulton, another American of Irish parentage, had built the *Nautilus*.

A further new weapon was the sea mine, employed successfully in the Crimean War by the Russians who had cone-shaped containers, about two feet deep and eighteen inches wide, holding gunpowder which would be detonated by the breaking of a glass tube full of acid. When David Bushnell of Saybrook, Connecticut, sent his little submarine, the *American Turtle* (she looked, he said, like the shells of two tortoises pressed together), against the British fleet at New York in 1776, the operator tried to fix a delayed-action bomb under Howe's flagship, the *Eagle*. From 1870 the underwater bomb was known as a mine, a name borrowed from the Army. Earlier it had been called a torpedo.

One development led to another. The mine demanded the minelayer and minesweeper as logically as the torpedo called for the torpedo boat, the torpedo-boat destroyer and the submarine, and no less predictably than the aircraft, in its turn, would inspire the aircraft carrier. The first true torpedo-boat destroyer, ancestor of the modern destroyer, the navy's ubiquitous maid-of-all-work, was HMS *Havock*, built by

Yarrow in 1893 as a craft of only 240 tons displacement with a low silhouette. Twin reciprocating engines propelled her at 27 knots. She carried a twelve-pounder gun and three six-pounders on her upper deck and was equipped with three torpedo tubes.

Designers had to concentrate more and more on specific functions. In 1866 Britain laid down the *Inconstant*, the first Royal Naval cruiser – an old word which had been used during the war between the States to denote a swift unarmoured vessel carrying sixteen ten-inch or eleven-inch smooth-bore guns. The following two decades brought in the armed cruiser, such as the *Warspite* of 1884, and the protected cruiser which had steel decks but no side armour.

Sir John Fisher's building programme for 1905–6 included the 17,900-ton *Dreadnought*, the most revolutionary ship since the *Devastation*. She mounted ten twelve-inch guns in five turrets, three of them on the fore-and-aft line and two abreast a little forward of amidships. Instead of the usual secondary armament she had 24 twelve-pounder quick-firing guns intended to repel torpedo attack. She could fire torpedoes herself, from five tubes of an improved type. Quadruple-screw turbines gave her a speed of 21.6 knots, making her about two knots faster than any other battleship, and she had a range of 5,800 nautical miles at cruising speed, or 3,500 at 18.5 knots. She was the first turbine ship in any navy. Her armour was extremely heavy and made of a new kind of steel.

The keel plate was laid on 2 October 1905 at

Above left: Launching of USS Nautilus. *On 17 January 1956 she sent out the historic signal: 'Under way on nuclear power'.*

Top right: HMS Devastation *of 1873, 'the first modern battleship'.*

Above right: Fairfield completed HMS Indomitable *in June 1908 as a battlecruiser designed to have 'a damned big six or seven knot surplus'.*

Below far left: Flight deck of US aircraft carrier Enterprise. *She is 1101½ ft long.*

Below near left: 'The Inflexible *in 1882 was a wonder', wrote Jacky Fisher who commanded her in the attacks on the Alexandria forts in that year.*

Portsmouth dockyard, and a year and a day later she was ready to go on her trials. It has been said again and again that she startled the world when Edward VII launched her on 10 February 1906. As the mightiest warship which had ever been built, she created a tremendous impression, but she did not take every government and navy department completely by surprise. Fisher had known in the spring of 1904 that Washington planned to build dreadnoughts, or their equivalent. Two of them, the *Michigan* and *South Carolina*, were authorized by Congress early in 1905; the fact that they were not completed until 1909 is irrelevant. As it was, the *Delaware* and *North Dakota* of 1907 outclassed the *Dreadnought*. They were followed by six others, all bearing, as a type, the name which had descended illustriously from the *Dreadnought*, one of the little ships ranged against the Spanish Armada.

In 1907 France and Germany each laid down four dreadnoughts, while Russia launched four and Italy five. Japan launched two, which mounted a dozen twelve-inch guns.

HMS *Dreadnought* made all earlier battleships obsolete. To the Design Committee headed by Prince Louis of Battenberg, father of Earl Mountbatten, it seemed logical that the same principle of all big-gun armament and high speed should be applied to the armoured cruiser. What the committee had in mind was a ship of about 17,000 tons displacement carrying eight twelve-inch guns and driven by turbines at 25 knots. Three such vessels, the *Invincible*, *Indomitable* and *Inflexible* were laid down in *Dreadnought* year. Owing to their speed and armament they had only medium armour protection. They were known at first as large armoured cruisers or fast battleships, and then, in 1911, as battleship cruisers before they came

to be listed, with their immediate successors, as battlecruisers, from 1912.

In 1905 Sir Percy Scott, then a rear-admiral, became the Admiralty's first Inspector of Target Practice. The contribution which he made to gunnery – 'he hits the target', Fisher said – was immense. After his retirement in 1909 he worked out a method of firing the main guns simultaneously from a control position high up in the foremast, clear of funnel smoke, cordite smoke and shell splashes. One man aimed the guns by using a master sight and then fired them by pressing a key. This director control, together with the formulation of spotting rules for observing the fall of shot, greatly improved the accuracy of fire at unprecedented ranges.

The British Admiralty had built the admired *Dreadnought* in the process of rescuing the Navy from a slough of inefficiency and lassitude. For many years past its ships had been largely engaged in maintaining the Pax Britannica; they had hunted pirates, fought the slave traders, carried out rescue work, charted the oceans and protected the far-flung countries of the Empire, often as a silent presence. Lacking the stimulus of any challenge greater than the Crimean War of 1853–6, the naval arm had grown drowsy and backward. An arch-conservatism flourished. The Navy was cursed with admirals and captains who delighted in intricate drills and abominated gunnery – ammunition was sometimes thrown overboard. They continued to think in terms of

the sailing navy; and there was indeed much to remind them of it, at least in the life of the lower deck. Yet the morale of the men was high. Since the introduction of long-term service in 1853 the poor tar had changed into the cheerful blue-jacket of popular legend.

It was fortunate for Britain and her Empire that the control of naval affairs passed, at a critical time, to Sir John Arbuthnot Fisher, appointed First Sea Lord on Trafalgar Day 1904. At the age of 63 this witty, vigorous, un-affected man, a great lover of sermons and dancing, directed the British Navy into a new age. Among other changes, he adopted the use of oil fuel and added submarines to the fleet when most naval officers despised them. Happily, he had the support of an intelligent public already awakened by Alfred Thayer Mahan to the importance of sea power. Mahan's thesis, ex-pounded in two books, was emphasized by the great naval review of 1897 for Queen Victoria's Jubilee and was given grim point by the naval race which had begun between Britain and the Germany of Wilhelm II.

The race culminated in August 1914. On 17 and 18 July at Spithead, the roadstead where the English ships had fought in 1545, the First Lord held a grand review which Churchill called 'incomparably the greatest assemblage of naval power ever witnessed in the history of the world'. Then, on the night of the 29th, the dark shapes of the First Fleet slipped up-channel on passage to Scapa Flow; and on 4 August at 11 pm, when the Kaiser's clocks were striking midnight, the Admiralty flashed a signal to all its ships: 'Commence hostilities against Ger-many.'

Britain entered the war with 20 dreadnoughts, 9 battlecruisers and 41 pre-dreadnoughts – if we include the *Lord Nelson* and *Agamemnon* ordered

in the 1904–5 programme and completed in 1908. Twelve more dreadnoughts and a battle-cruiser were under construction. In 1915 Britain was to have, among the twelve battleships, the five splendid oil-fired, fifteen-inch-gun vessels of the Queen Elizabeth class, the *Queen Elizabeth*, *Warspite*, *Barham*, *Valiant* and *Malaya*, re-nowned in both World Wars.

The Admiralty also acquired five brand-new battleships from British yards, the *Almirante Lattore* (renamed the *Canada*), built for Chile, and the *Sultan Osman I* and *Reshadieh* (after-wards HMS *Agincourt* and HMS *Erin*) intended for the Turks – who came in on the side of the Kaiser after the Germans had let them have the battlecruiser *Goeben* and the light cruiser *Breslau*, which had raced away from the British battle-cruisers *Indomitable* and *Inflexible* on the first day of war, to reach Constantinople and become the *Yavuz* and *Midilli*. The *Yavuz* survived into the 1970s.

There were thirteen dreadnoughts and five

Above: 'The Emden *beached and done for' by Arthur Burgess. Von Müller's raider was sunk off the Cocos Islands on 9 November 1914 by the Australian cruiser* Sydney.

Below: Throughout both World Wars there was a tradition in the Royal Navy that if an action was to be fought the Warspite *would be there – and in the thick of it. The 27,500-ton battleship was launched in 1913. In 1947 she broke away from her tugs on the way to shipbreakers and went aground near Penzance in Cornwall. 'When the old lady lifts her skirts she can still run,' Admiral of the Fleet Lord Cunningham of Hyndhope once testified.*

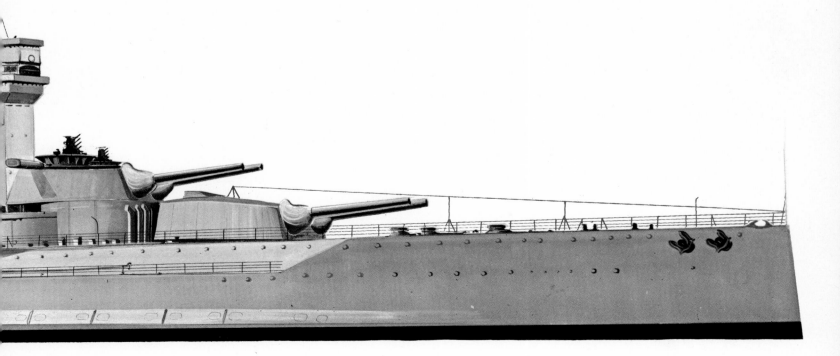

battlecruisers in the German fleet (if we add the *Blücher*, which had twelve 8.2-inch guns). Seven more dreadnoughts and three battlecruisers were under construction.

It was commonly supposed that sooner or later the fleets would be locked decisively. But when at last they met, off the Jutland peninsula in the North Sea on 31 May 1916, the results were inconclusive and disappointed both sides. The British Grand Fleet under Admiral Sir John Jellicoe – the only man, observed Churchill, who could have lost the war in an afternoon – had three battlecruisers sunk (the *Queen Mary* and *Indefatigable* of David Beatty's squadron and the *Invincible* in the Third Battle Squadron under Horace Hood) and also three heavy cruisers and eight destroyers. Together they

Above: The German armed cruiser Scharnhorst *of 11,600 tons was built in 1906 at Hamburg by Blohm and Voss. She was sunk with all hands in 1914 at the Battle of the Falkland Islands. Her namesake of the Second World War, completed in 1938 with an actual displacement of 31,800 tons, was sunk in 1943 off North Cape.*

Right: Among the modern attractions of Leningrad is the Russian cruiser Aurora, *preserved in recognition of her part in the October Revolution of 1917.*

represented twice the tonnage of the German ships eliminated: one battleship (the old *Pommern*), one battlecruiser (the *Lützow*) and four light cruisers and five destroyers. The British casualties were 6,000 compared with Admiral Reinhardt Scheer's 2,500. None the less Britain remained indisputably mistress of the seas. 'The German fleet', remarked an American commentator, 'has assaulted its jailer, but it is still in jail.'

Having been denied supremacy on the surface, the Germans turned to unrestricted warfare by their underwater craft. In April 1917 the total of merchant shipping lost, including neutral vessels, rose to 875,000 tons. It was in that month that America joined the Allies. The convoy system, familiar from the past, was belatedly put into operation while the United States worked on a building programme which included 272 destroyers and a great many smaller anti-submarine vessels. Before most of them had

been completed, the war was over. In the end, on the sunny morning of 21 June 1919, the 74 vessels of Alfred von Tirpitz' High Seas Fleet disappeared beneath the waters of Scapa Flow, scuttled by their skeleton crews. Many great deeds had been accomplished. In time to come the story would be told again and again of Von Spee at Coronel and Doveton Sturdee at the Falklands, of Roger Keyes and the raid on Zeebrugge, of Karl von Müller and the lone raider *Emden* which in 70 days captured 23 ships, worth an estimated £2,200,000, before she met the Australian light cruiser *Sydney* north of the Cocos Islands.

After the war, in 1922, Great Britain, the United States, France, Italy and Japan signed the Five-Power Naval Treaty intended to avert another building race. 'There is only one way out,' declared Charles Evans Hughes, the American Secretary of State at the Conference in Washington, 'and that is to end it now.' Great Britain was to retain 22 capital ships of 580,000 tons in all; the United States 18 of 500,000;

Japan 10 of 301,000; France 10 of 221,000; and Italy 10 of 182,000. In addition, the British Empire would scrap 23 ships of 583,375 tons, the United States 30 of 845,740, and Japan 17 of 448,928.

Tragically, nothing averted another war. It found Germany with seven very powerful war-ships, not one of which remained in German hands at the end of hostilities. The pocket battle-ship *Admiral Graf Spee* was blown up by Captain Langsdorff after the Battle of the River Plate; the battleship *Bismarck* sank in battle after she had been hit by torpedoes from *Ark Royal* aircraft; the battlecruiser *Scharnhorst* was destroyed by a mixed force under Admiral Fraser (now Admiral of the Fleet Lord Fraser of North Cape) in the Arctic; the battleship *Tirpitz* met her end in Tromsø Fjord; the battlecruiser *Gneisenau* was taken by the Russians at Gdynia, to be used as a blockship; and the pocket battle-ships *Admiral Scheer* and *Lützow* (formerly the *Deutschland*) were lost in the heavy bombings of 1945 at Kiel and Swinemünde.

Above left: HMS Hood *leaving Clydebank in 1920. 'The Mighty* Hood' *was completed in March of that year as a battlecruiser of 41,200 tons displacement. In the action with the Bismarck on 24 May 1941, she blew up with the loss of all but three of her company after being struck by a salvo.*

Below far left: The Ark Royal *in wartime.*

Below near left: The scene on the deck of the Ark Royal *minutes before she was sunk by a U-boat on 14 November 1941.*

Below: USS King, *guided missile cruiser, in San Diego Bay.*

89,600-ton nuclear-powered *Enterprise* in 1961. Vessels of this size were a far cry indeed from the seaplane carrier *Engadine* from which had been launched the little aeroplane at Jutland. Perhaps they were too big; in 1975, when the $1,000,000 *Nimitz*, a floating town with a population of over 5,000, paid her first visit to Britain, the United States began to study the possible advantages of having smaller, cheaper carriers.

As British carriers had proved their worth, not least in the Pacific, naval circles were astonished and indignant when the authorities cancelled the building of new carriers. Instead of having carriers the Royal Navy would depend upon the anti-submarine or through-deck cruiser (sometimes called, jokingly or by accident, the 'see-through cruiser') and the maritime version of the Harrier jump-jet, the aircraft which takes off and lands vertically. The prototype, to be named HMS *Invincible*, was laid down at Barrow-in-Furness on 20 July 1973.

With the end of the Second World War, the trident had passed from Great Britain to the United States, which possessed the largest fleet in history. Before long the American supremacy was challenged. The leaders in the Kremlin, behaving exactly as though they too had been reading Mahan, were intent on making the USSR an ocean superpower. Whenever the Royal Navy began an exercise, a few Soviet trawlers appeared out of nowhere. It was stated in 1975 that Russian nuclear-propelled killer submarines were 'three times as numerous' as the U-boats in the Second World War, and that the latest Russian missile destroyers and cruisers were 'five years ahead of the best of their Nato counterparts', and would shortly be joined by the first of a fleet of aircraft carriers.

By this time the world's navies had been transformed by science and technology. In the Royal Navy the old conservatism had given way to an attitude of mind which eagerly accepted the latest gifts of research and invention. The radio of the First World War and the radar (at first a British secret) and asdic, or sonar, of the Second marked the beginning of a revolution embracing nuclear propulsion, the gas turbine and a vast intricacy of electronic apparatus operated by highly-trained specialists in such vessels as guided-missile ships, general-purpose frigates, anti-aircraft frigates, air-direction frigates, anti-submarine frigates, submarines (some of them nuclear-powered, some also carrying the Polaris missile) and destroyers, minehunters and other modern descendants of the *Revenge* and *Sovereign of the Seas*. There was an occasion when British warships leaving on exercises were described as 'HM Computers proceeding to sea'. But if the old naval life belongs to the past and the young sailor of today has to be told that grog was the daily rum ration, much of what was best in the great tradition remains.

Top: The submarine Resolution.

Above left: A Polaris submarine carries ballistic missiles of that name and fires them from underwater. When the US submarine George Washington *fired two consecutive missiles from a submerged position off Cape Kennedy in 1960, the range was 1,200 miles.*

Above right: HMAS Sydney *in action off Crete during World War II.*

Right: The US aircraft carrier Nimitz *has a crew of more than 5,000.*

Following pages: Two frigates of the Royal Navy, Antelope *and* Amazon.

Losses on the British side included the battleship *Royal Oak*, torpedoed at Scapa Flow with a death toll of over 800; the old battlecruiser *Hood*, sunk by the *Bismarck* with only three survivors from her complement of 1,418; the battleship *Barham*, torpedoed and blown up off the Egyptian coast; the battleship *Prince of Wales* and the battlecruiser *Repulse*, sunk by Japanese air attack off Malaya; and five aircraft carriers, the *Courageous, Glorious, Ark Royal, Eagle* and *Hermes*. Anti-submarine duties made huge demands of the Royal Navy; the Battle of the Atlantic and the Russian convoys had an epic quality, humdrum though much of the work was for those involved. Allied failure in the Atlantic would have meant utter defeat.

The war in the Pacific, fought on an immense scale, sealed the fate of the battleship. It was generally accepted that the capital ship of the future would be the aircraft carrier. Planning accordingly, the United States produced the

Great Ocean Liners

NO ONE CAN STUDY the life of colonial America without being impressed by the extent of the traffic between the New World and the Old. The little ship *Arbella*, taking across the leaders of the Massachusetts Bay colony in 1630, ten years after the *Mayflower* sailed, led a continuous migration.

Having settled in America, the immigrants relied upon ships from England for a great variety of merchandise – everything which they could not grow or make themselves – and some of them also kept a more personal contact with the homeland, crossing for business or pleasure, or sending their sons across to the universities of Oxford and Cambridge. By the eighteenth century the 'news of Virginia' was a familiar topic in the London coffee houses, and throughout the nineteenth century a strong Atlantic culture was in flower. Americans followed the Washington Irving trail to Stratford-upon-Avon, and Dickens went to America at Irving's invitation; Ralph Waldo Emerson called on Wordsworth in the Lake District; Fanny Kemble, the actress, was impressed by Niagara; Harriet Beecher Stowe, the author of *Uncle Tom's Cabin*, regretted that she could never again visit Sir Walter Scott's country for the *first* time. Yet even the best passages were grimly uncomfortable, at least by the standards of today. Until the 1830s the crowded ships were propelled by the same capricious power that had taken Sir Richard Grenville's colonists to Roanoke in 1585 and the *Susan Constant, Godspeed* and *Discovery* to the James River in 1607. Voyages were long and uncertain; a vessel might be weeks beating her way down Channel from the Thames or waiting for a favourable wind.

The Black Ball Line, founded at New York in 1816, brought the first big improvement by shortening the period of discomfort. It boasted an average passage of 40 days from Liverpool to New York and 23 days back to Liverpool.

Running in competition with the packets of the Swallow Tail Line, the Black Star, the Red Star, the Black X, the White Diamond and the Dramatic, the Black Ball vessels sailed on time whether they were packed or empty; one of them left New York for Liverpool on the first and sixteenth of every month.

When the ship berthed, none of the new arrivals was happier than those travelling steerage. While first-class passengers drank whisky and played cards like travellers in Mississippi and Ohio steamboats, poor emigrants huddled in semi-darkness, enduring frightful discomforts and miseries, and sometimes agonies too. Most of the passengers had no intention of returning, except perhaps on a visit when they had found their crock of gold. According to the official figures, over 2,300,000 immigrants crossed to America from the British Isles in the ten years from 1846 to 1855.

In 1838 two Nova Scotians, Judge Thomas Haliburton and Joseph Howe, were 20 days out of Halifax on a visit to England when their ship met the paddle steamer *Sirius*. The little steamship, said Howe, approached 'with the speed of a hunter, while we were moving with the rapidity of an ox-cart loaded with marsh mud'. It can hardly have been an accident that in November of that year another leading Haligonian, Samuel Cunard, a devout Quaker whose forebears had emigrated to Philadelphia in 1683, answered an Admiralty request for steamships capable of maintaining a monthly mail service across the Atlantic. After two of his tenders had been rejected, he left for England.

By an agreement made on 11 February 1839, he undertook to provide three steamships and to incorporate, during the continuance of the contract, 'any improvements in Steam Navigation' which the heads of the Admiralty might consider essential. He then called on James C. Melvill, Secretary of the East India Company for advice as to who could build the three ships. Without hesitation, Melvill recommended Robert Napier, a brilliant marine engineer who

*Opposite previous page:
The second* Mauretania
*(35,738 tons). She was
built by Cammell Laird,
Birkenhead for Cunard in
1939. After being laid up at
New York for three months
she sailed to Cockatoo
Island, Sydney, and was
converted into a troopship.
She was scrapped in 1965.*

*Right: Reconstruction of
the 1620* Mayflower *by
Stuart Upham of Brixham
in Devon to the plans of the
American ship designer
William Baker. In 1957
Alan Villiers sailed her
from Plymouth, Devon, to
Plymouth Rock, New
England.*

Below: The P & O ship
Britannia *of 1887. She was
one of four 6,500-ton,
15-knot liners built by the
company in 1887 and 1888
for the Australian route to
celebrate the Golden
Jubilee of Queen Victoria
and the P & O. The other
three were the* Victoria,
Oceana *and* Arcadia. *For a
short time they carried sails
as well as using steam.*

designed and built the machinery for hulls constructed by his partner, John Wood.

In March 1839, Samuel Cunard and Robert Napier met for the first time. Out of that meeting grew the great and famous Cunard Steamship Company. The problem of finance was solved when Napier called in George Burns, owner of coastal steamships, and David McIver, his Liverpool agent. Within a few days 32 businessmen had subscribed £270,000, more than enough capital to build the three ships required by the Admiralty and another vessel as well, the head postmaster at Quebec having suggested that with four ships the service could have fixed departure days on both sides of the Atlantic. The line was first known as 'The British and North American Royal Mail Steam-Packet Company'.

Writing to Melvill about Cunard on 18 March, Napier had said: 'From the frank off-hand manner in which he contracted with me, I have given him the vessels cheap, and I am certain they will be good and very strong ships.' The four were the *Britannia* of 1840 and her sister ships, the *Acadia*, *Caledonia* and the *Columbia*.

At Liverpool the *Britannia* had to be swung out into midstream 'owing to her immense size'. She was 228ft long overall and 34.3ft in beam (56ft over the paddle boxes) with a mean draught of 16.8ft and a gross tonnage of 1,156. Two side-lever engines of 740 indicated horsepower turned her 28ft paddle wheels at sixteen revolutions a minute and gave her a normal speed of about 8.5 knots. Leaving Liverpool on 4 July 1840, she crossed to Halifax in eleven days four hours at a mean speed of ten knots and completed her run to Boston in fourteen days eight hours.

Her accommodation – the dining saloon and cabins for 115 on the main deck below – was described as luxurious.

When the *Britannia* was gripped by ice seven feet thick at Boston on 1 February 1844, residents cut a passage seven miles long and 100 feet wide to free her. She left on 3 February, only two days late, followed by cheering citizens in sleighs and 'sailing boats fitted up with long blades of iron like skates'. Bostonians were proud of the *Britannia*, and they did not want her to call at New York instead on the grounds that the sea there was less likely to freeze.

The Cunard company did not lack competitors. At the outset the Great Western Steamship Company at Bristol had expected to receive the mail contract as the owners of the only fully effective Atlantic steamship, Brunel's *Great Western*. When the Admiralty accepted Samuel Cunard's tender, Brunel began work on the *Great Britain*. But she took six years to build, and by the time she went into service the Cunard Line was firmly established. She did not remain long on the Atlantic, as we shall see (Chapter 4).

Samuel Cunard met his first serious challenge when Edward Knight Collins from Cape Cod,

after running the Dramatic Line of sailing packets, turned to steamships. He was not one to do things by halves. His first packet had been the *Shakespeare*, the largest merchant ship that had ever flown the American flag; and his *Atlantic* of 1849 was a beautiful wooden steamship of 2,860 tons which set new standards in comfort and speed. Contracting with the United States Government to operate a subsidized mail service between New York and Liverpool every two weeks for eight months of the year and monthly in the winter, he devoted himself to 'the absolute conquest of this man Cunard' by offering the Atlantic travellers a fast voyage in a ship which boasted such luxuries as steam heat, bathrooms (Cunard passengers were hosed down on request), ice, a barber's shop, a proper smoking room, and two main saloons panelled

Above left: The P & O Jubilee ship Victoria. *In later years she was often on the Bombay run. She was scrapped in 1909.*

Above: Inman's City of New York *passes Bowling on the Clyde.*

in expensive woods and furnished with sofas and upholstered chairs resting on deep carpet. The menu in the dining room, a space 60 feet long and 20 wide, suggested a first-class hotel on shore.

So attractive were the Collins liners that in 1851 they carried three passengers for every two travelling with Cunard. The *Atlantic, Pacific, Baltic* and *Arctic* won the distinction later known as the Blue Riband; but the speed of the Collins vessels was dearly bought. It has been said that they shook themselves to pieces: at New York mechanics worked day and night on repairs.

Off Cape Race on 27 September 1854 the *Arctic* went down with the loss of 322 lives after a collision in dense fog with the small French steamer *Vesta*, the crew of which took to the boats, not knowing that it was the other ship which had received by far the worse damage. Among the casualties were the wife, son and daughter of Edward Collins. As though this were not misfortune enough, his *Pacific* vanished

without trace in 1856. In the following year he acquired the 3,670-ton *Adriatic*, remembered as the last and biggest wooden paddle steamer to be built for the North Atlantic. She cost over a million dollars, a vast sum at any time in the nineteenth century, but she was too late to save the Collins Line from bankruptcy despite a subsidy from Congress.

The next important arrival on the Atlantic scene, William Inman of Liverpool, also lost two ships. In March 1854 his 1,600-ton *City of Glasgow*, an iron-hulled screw steamer built by Tod and McGregor, sailed from Liverpool with 480 on board and was never heard of again, and in the summer his new 2,200-ton *City of Philadelphia* was wrecked, without loss of life, off Cape Race. Nevertheless his company prospered. In the last 27 years of his life his ships carried more than a million emigrants to the United States. All the vessels had names beginning with 'City of'. In 1867 the 2,650-ton *City of Paris* made the passage from Queenstown to New York in eight days four hours, a record not broken for another five years. The 8,400-ton *City of Rome* set a fashion as the first three-

Left: The Palm Court of the Majestic. *The White Star liner was launched on 20 June 1914 as the* Bismarck *of the Hamburg-American Line. In 1936 she became the training ship* Caledonia. *Three years later she was gutted by fire at Rosyth in Scotland.*

Above: The first-class dining room of a Greenock-built liner believed to be the Orinoco *constructed in 1886 for the West Indian service of the Royal Mail Line.*

Right: Brunel's Great Western. *She made her first Atlantic crossing in April 1838. She was built at Bristol by William Patterson as a steamship of 1,320 tons, 236 feet long overall. Her paddle-wheels were 28.75 feet in diameter with fixed floats 10 feet long. They made 15 revolutions a minute. The mean speed on the first crossing was 8.8 knots, the ship arriving at New York in 15 days 5 hours.*

funnelled liner in the trade, but the company was dissatisfied and her builders sold her to the Anchor Line, which at one stage ran a twice-weekly service between Glasgow and New York. Eventually the Inman Line itself passed into other hands – the American International Navigation Company.

Competition was increasing. In 1870 the line founded by Stephen Barker Guion, formerly head of Cunard's new steerage department, had seven Atlantic passenger vessels. On a voyage in 1879 its 5,150-ton *Arizona* put into St John's, Newfoundland, after striking an iceberg – excellent proof, the Victorians said, that Guion ships could be trusted. The Guion *Oregon*, which crossed from Queenstown to New York in six days and ten hours, was the fastest vessel afloat. When the company failed, Cunard took her over and benefited accordingly.

Cunard competitors came and went; but the Oceanic Steamship Company, the White Star Line, founded by Thomas Henry Ismay from Maryport in Cumberland, opened a battle of giants which did not end until the British Government compelled them to unite in 1934.

White Star suffered two frightful tragedies. In April 1873, after a week of appalling weather, the *Atlantic* changed course for Halifax on her way to New York, the engineer having incorrectly reported that she was running out of coal. Off Meagher's Head, near the Canadian port, she struck some notorious rocks and was wrecked with the loss of 562 lives. The disaster was the grimmest ever recorded in the Atlantic trade until that other April 39 years later when White Star's 'unsinkable' *Titanic* ran into an iceberg and 1,494 people died.

However much the Cunard vessels might be outclassed at various periods in speed and comfort, they possessed one superlative virtue. They were as safe as skill and care could make them. 'The Cunard people', testified Mark

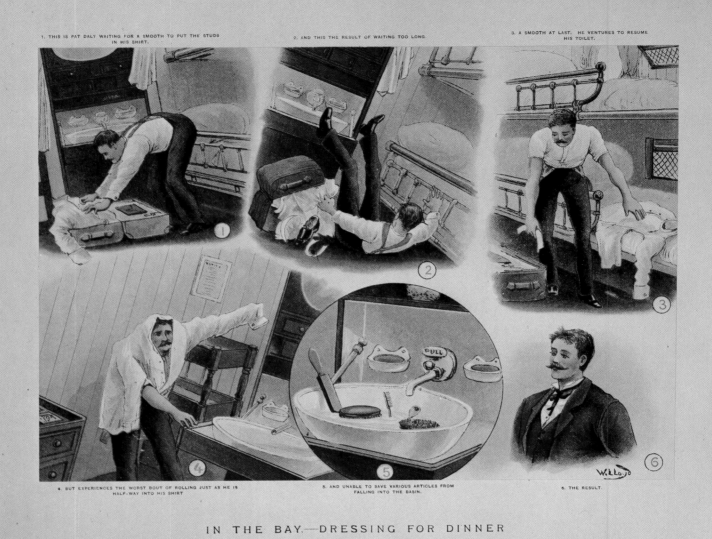

1. THIS IS PAT DALY WAITING FOR A SMOOTH TO PUT THE STUDS IN HIS SHIRT.

2. AND THIS THE RESULT OF WAITING TOO LONG.

3. A SMOOTH AT LAST. HE VENTURES TO RESUME HIS TOILET.

4. BUT EXPERIENCES THE WORST BOUT OF ROLLING JUST AS HE IS HALF-WAY INTO HIS SHIRT

5. AND UNABLE TO SAVE VARIOUS ARTICLES FROM FALLING INTO THE BASIN.

6. THE RESULT.

IN THE BAY.—DRESSING FOR DINNER

Twain, 'would not take on Noah himself as first mate till they had worked him up through all the lower grades and tried him ten years on such matter.'

Cunard's last paddle steamer was the *Scotia*, which in 1864 reduced the time for the New York–Queenstown run to eight days four hours. She remained a favourite for many years after the introduction in 1862 of the first screw Cunarder, the *China*. The company's first iron vessel, the *Persia* of 1855, proved a record breaker, and its first steel ship, the *Servia* of 1881, was a pioneer in the full use of electric light on board a liner.

Great Britain and the United States did not have the Atlantic to themselves. Several other countries made a bid for a share of the traffic. Adopting steam, the Hamburg–America Line ordered the 2,000-ton *Hammonia* and *Borussia* of 1855. No one can have been surprised when the rival port of Bremen also entered the Atlantic trade. Its new company, Norddeutscher-Lloyd, began with four steamers laid down in Britain. Hamburg was not pleased to see the first of them, the 2,500-ton *Bremen* of 1858, advertised as having 'made the quickest passage on record'. Long afterwards, in the 1880s, the Hamburg-America Line profited greatly from the enterprise of Albert Ballin, but it was North German Lloyd which ordered the 4,350-ton *Kaiser Wilhelm der Grosse*, proudly launched in the year of Queen Victoria's Diamond Jubilee as a ship which made the Cunard Line look out of date. With her band playing jubilantly, she crossed the Atlantic at 22 knots. She was the largest and

fastest liner on the seas.

In 1875 Inman gained the record for both directions with the 16-knot *City of Berlin*, built by Caird's; but in the same period Harland and Wolff completed two 16-knot, 5,000-ton ships, the *Britannic* and *Germanic*, for its regular customer the White Star Line. They were designed as improvements on the White Star *Oceanic* and both made records.

New times for both directions were set again in 1884 by the 5,500-ton *America* of the National Line, a 432ft steel vessel, schooner-rigged, and with two lofty elliptical funnels and a clipper stem. She was soon beaten by the *Oregon* which ran as consort for the famous *Etruria* and *Umbria*; until she was lost in collision near Fire Island off New York on 14 March 1886. Within the space of a few years the speed honours passed from Cunard to Inman and International, to White Star, and then to Inman again, before Cunard wrested them back. After the success of the 22-knot *Wilhelm der Grosse*, which had four funnels arranged in two pairs, Hamburg-America replied with the rather similar *Deutschland*. She vibrated badly and cost so much to maintain that Hamburg-America withdrew from the competition and left its old Bremen rivals to rejoice in the triumphs of the *Kronprinz Wilhelm* and *Kaiser Wilhelm II*.

In the era of fierce competition before the First World War, J. Pierpont Morgan gave the United States a bigger slice of the Atlantic cake by bringing White Star and several other British lines into his International Mercantile Marine Company, an intricate concern founded in 1902. The rivalry between I.M.M. and Cunard, which

had not let itself be caught in the Morgan net, reached a point that in 1904 a person could cross the Western Ocean for 30s., or $7.50.

During that period, when thousands were accepting the invitation from the Statue of Liberty – 'Send me your tired, your poor, Your huddled masses yearning to breathe free' – the Holland-America Line, after losing six of its best ships in the 1880s and 1890s, launched the *Potsdam*, *Noordam* and *Ryndam*, all of 12,500

Above far left: The hazards of travelling at sea.

Below far left: North German Lloyd's Kaiser Wilhelm der Grosse *of 1897.*

Below centre left: Pacific record-breaker, the 16,810-ton Empress of Russia.

Top right: The 'unsinkable' Titanic, *built by Harland and Wolff at Belfast for the White Star Line and launched on 31 May 1911. Near midnight on 14 April 1912 her maiden voyage to New York ended in horror when she struck an iceberg and sank.*

Above right: The lounge of the Lusitania. *Ever since 1915 she has lain on the sea-bed off the Irish coast near the Old Head of Kinsale, Co Cork.*

Near left: 'In the Stokehold'.

Above: The ill-fated Lusitania. She was built by John Brown's for Cunard in 1907 as a turbine ship of 31,550 tons. She began her maiden voyage to New York from Liverpool on 7 September 1907 and soon recaptured the Atlantic speed record for Britain. While making for England on 7 May 1915, she was sunk by a U-boat with the loss of 1,198 lives.

Right: In 1950 the much-loved Aquitania was turned into scrap in the Gareloch, an inlet of the Clyde, after a career of 36 years, in the course of which she had crossed the Atlantic about 600 times. She was a Cunarder of 45,647 tons built by John Brown's and launched on 23 April 1913. She was a troopship in both World Wars and an armed merchant cruiser in 1914.

Far right: Dancing on deck in the Aquitania.

tons, the *Nieuw Amsterdam* of 17,000 tons, and then the 24,000-ton *Rotterdam*, which remained on its register from 1908 to 1940. In half a century on the Atlantic the Dutch had made 1,300 voyages and carried 130,000 passengers, 40,000 of whom travelled steerage.

Another country with Atlantic ambitions was Canada. It was natural that when the Canadian Pacific Railway had been completed, the company should take the route still further by sea. Having sent its first stately Empresses across the Pacific, it turned its attention to the Western Ocean. In 1903 it bought the Canadian assets of Elder Dempster, to which it added, during the First World War, the resourceful and reliable Allan Line.

Helped by the British Government, the Cunard company met every challenge coolly

enough. It launched the 'pretty sisters' *Caronia* and *Carmania* in 1905, and the magnificent *Lusitania* with her sister ship the *Mauretania* in 1907. Both these 30,000-tonners were record breakers, designed to fill the need for two vessels easily convertible into armed merchant cruisers if war came. They reduced the Atlantic crossing to less than five days, about the same time that the *United States* and the *Queens* would take half a century later.

The *Mauretania*, holder of the Blue Riband for a total of 22 years, inspired warm affection. 'Every ship has a soul,' said Franklin D. Roosevelt. 'But the *Mauretania* has one you can talk to.' She was joined in 1914 by another much-loved ship, the 45,647-ton *Aquitania*. For many years past shipowners and naval architects had done their best to convince the passenger that he was still ashore – and not only ashore but in extremely comfortable or palatial surroundings. The *Aquitania* enhanced this reputation; according to a shipbuilder's journal, her decoration was inspired by Holbein, van Dyck, Inigo Jones, Wren, the Adams brothers and the 'French masters who flourished in the early part of the reign of Louis the Magnificent'.

There came a time when adornments meant nothing. In August 1914 the *Aquitania* was converted into an armed merchant cruiser. She then became a hospital ship and afterwards a troopcarrier, a duty which she performed again

in the Second World War. By the time she went for scrap in 1950 she had crossed the Atlantic about 600 times.

In the South Atlantic on 14 September 1914 the 'pretty' *Carmania* fought and sank the Hamburg-America *Cap Trafalgar*, an armed merchant cruiser like herself, and formerly the pride of Hamburg-America's South American service. The worst loss among liners was Britain's: the sinking of the *Lusitania*, bound from New York, by the *U20* off the Irish coast on 7 May 1915. In eighteen minutes 1,198 people died.

After the war a number of former German liners became famous on the Atlantic under new names. The *Imperator* of 1912 joined the Cunard fleet as the *Berengaria*, the *Bismarck* was completed as the White Star *Majestic* and the *Columbus* as the *Homeric*, while the *Vaterland*, seized by America in 1917, went to the United States Lines, descended from the American Steamship Company of 1873 as the *Leviathan*. All were Hamburg vessels of over 50,000 tons.

In France the Compagnie Générale Transatlantique also had a ship to complete – its own 34,570-ton *Paris*, which had been launched in 1916 and then towed to Quiberon Bay. This luxurious and beautifully decorated liner ran with the four-funnelled *France* of 1912 on the Le Havre–New York express service. In 1927 the French Line added the *Ile de France*, an elegant new vessel of 43,150 tons. American

travellers in the 1920s were particularly fond of the French Line.

It was not long before the Germans returned to the passenger business. Their 51,650-ton *Bremen* of 1928, the fourth of her name, captured the Blue Riband from the *Mauretania*. Atlantic liners were becoming symbols of national prestige. In the 1930s Mussolini ordered the building of two great ships, the *Rex* and the *Conte di Savoia*, both of which were set on fire by Allied

Overleaf: The rusting hulk of the Queen Elizabeth *(or Seawise University) in Hong Kong harbour where she was destroyed by fire on 9 January 1972.*

aircraft during the Second World War.

The spirit of the twenties was at its gayest on board the Atlantic liners. They might have been designed for Scott Fitzgerald characters in search of a long, jazzy house party. Americans headed for Paris; Britons set out to see for themselves the 'cloud-capt' towers of Manhattan. No people were better at creating the required atmosphere of light-hearted adventure than the French. Carrying the mood into the thirties, the C.G.T. launched one of the most beautiful liners ever commissioned, the 79,280-ton turbo-electric *Normandie*.

Joining the *Ile de France, Paris, Lafayette, Champlain* and *De Grasse*, she opened her Atlantic career by crossing from Bishop Rock to Ambrose Light in four days and three hours. The outbreak of war found her at New York, where she remained. In February 1942 the United States authorities were converting her into a troopship when a blow lamp set alight to some bedding on board. Becoming top-heavy from the thousands of gallons of water directed on her by the Fire Department hoses, she heeled over and sank. What remained of her was fit only for the scrapyard.

The biggest and most famous liner of all was born in the shadows of the Great Depression. On 26 September 1934, Hull 534 at John Brown's yard on the Clyde was transformed into the *Queen Mary* as the Queen herself broke a bottle of Australian wine – champagne of course is *French* – against her bows. From John Brown's yard the new wonder of the age moved grandly into the River Cart, a Cunarder of 80,774 tons, 1,018ft long overall. Unaided by computers, the Press set out to astonish its readers with ingenious calculations. The tonnage of the *Queen Mary*, they learnt, exceeded by more than 20,000 that of the entire Spanish Armada. The *Britannia* of 1840 and Columbus's three ships, the *Santa Maria, Niña* and *Pinta*, could all have berthed in her main dining room and foyer, and there was enough electric cable inside her to reach from New York to San Francisco and eight hundred miles further towards Hawaii – a total of four thousand miles.

It was announced at the launching that she would have a sister ship and that the pair would 'battle for victory in the international struggle on the North Atlantic'. The struggle turned out to be far different from the competition that the Cunard company had in mind. On 30 August 1939 the *Queen Mary* put out from Southampton with 2,332 passengers, and before she arrived at New York the British were at war.

The promised sister ship, No. 552, the 83,675-ton *Queen Elizabeth*, had been laid down on 4 December 1936 and launched by the consort of King George VI (now Queen Elizabeth the Queen Mother). For a time the new liner lay uncompleted in the Clyde while John Brown's

Right: Last moments of the Andrea Doria, *the luxurious Italian liner of 29,082 tons sunk in collision off Nantucket on the morning of 26 July 1956.*

Below: The Queen Elizabeth *as a troopship.*

Bottom: The Mauretania

Top far right: The Spirit of France.

Centre far right: The 48,502-ton Italian liner Conte di Savoia.

Bottom right: The 52,226-ton Berengaria.

yard concentrated on fitting out the battleship *Duke of York*; and then, after huge packing cases had been sent to Southampton and hotel rooms had been booked there for Cunard technicians who would never arrive, she crossed the Atlantic like a grey ghost. On the morning of 7 March 1940 the crew of a TWA airliner over the New York area saw a tremendous ship zigzagging swiftly towards the harbour. The *Queen Elizabeth* was about to keep her secret appointment with the *Queen Mary* at Pier 90. 'Many sagas of the sea have begun and ended in our harbour,' said the *New York Times*, 'but can the old-timers remember anything to compare with the unheralded arrival of the biggest and fastest liner in the world, after the most daring of all maiden crossings?'

In company with other liners the *Queens* divested themselves of everything luxurious and sailed as troopships. On 5 May 1940 the first 5,000 troops went on board the *Queen Mary* at Sydney to be given wooden bunks for the voyage. Both ships later ferried troops from America.

Above: The elegant liner Guglielmo Marconi, *built at Trieste in 1963 with a gross tonnage of 27,905.*

Above right: The Queen Elizabeth II, *the Cunarder of 66,851 tons built in 1968 as an Atlantic liner and a cruise ship.*

Below: Thousands of people have happy memories of educational cruises in the Uganda *(16,907 tons), built for the British India Steam Navigation Company by Barclay, Curle of Glasgow in 1952.*

In April 1941 they were on the open sea together for the first time, reunited in an ocean for which they had never been intended. With the end of the fighting, the *Queen Mary* was given a more pleasant task: between February and May 1946 she took 9,118 wives and 3,768 children to their new homes in North America. Only one incident darkened the record of the two great ships in wartime: the accidental ramming of the HMS *Curacoa* by the *Queen Mary* 40 miles north of Tory Island, Donegal, on 2 October 1942 when the former liner was zigzagging her way to the Clyde with 15,000 American troops on board. The cruiser was struck on her port quarter abaft the engine room. While the engineers in the *Queen Mary* felt only a slight jolt, the cruiser broke in two and sank within five minutes, taking with her 338 men.

During the war the *Queen Mary* and *Queen Elizabeth* carried a total of 1,243,538 troops. On the North Atlantic they transported 869,694 troops eastbound and 213,008 westbound, a total of 1,082,702. 'To the men who contributed to the success of operations in the years of peril,' declared Winston Churchill, 'and to those who brought these two great ships into existence, the world owes a debt that it will not be easy to measure.'

The war had begun with the sinking of a liner.

On the very first day, Sunday 3 September 1939, the 13,465-ton *Athenia* of the Anchor-Donaldson Line, outward bound for North America, was torpedoed by Korvetten-Kapitan Lemp's *U110* two hundred miles west of the Hebrides. One of the survivors remembers nothing more vividly than the sudden dead silence after a terrific jolt which threw her against a deck-rail. 'All we knew at first,' she says, 'was that the engines had stopped. We did not realize immediately that a torpedo had struck the ship and she was sinking. I had been watching the sun go down and trying to absorb the news, which had reached us in the morning, that Britain and Germany were at war. We did not expect it to begin with ourselves, on the wide ocean. It is strange now to think that the U-boat commander was a young man of about my own age'.

There were other liner casualties as the war continued. Holland-America's *Statendam* was burnt on 14 May 1940 during the fighting in Rotterdam; the *Empress of Britain*, running as a troopship, was torpedoed by *U32* on 28 October 1940, after an air attack; the *Champlain* of the French Line was blown up by a magnetic mine off La Rochelle on 17 June in the same year. Italy lost two handsome ships of 32,000 tons: the *Augustus*, scuttled by the Germans at Genoa in 1944 after the Italian armistice, and the *Roma*, attacked by British and Italian frogmen when she was already in German hands as the aircraft carrier *Aquila*.

A superb liner laid down after the return of

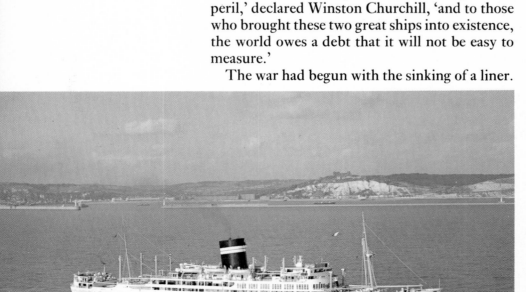

sixties was the 51,840-ton *Liberté*, formerly North German Lloyd's *Europa* of 1930. On board the *Liberté* one was content to eat, laze, eat and laze again. By the time that she went to shipbreakers at Spezia in 1962, the 66,350-ton *France* was afloat as a worthy successor to the lost *Normandie*. She was the longest liner in the world and the most elegant. For about seven years she shared the Atlantic ferry with the *United States*. In July 1952 this 53,330-ton American superliner had set a new eastbound record of three days ten hours and forty minutes and a new westbound record of three days twelve hours and twelve minutes on her first voyage out and home.

A brand new Cunarder was launched by the Queen on 20 September 1967. She was the 66,851-ton twin-screw *Queen Elizabeth II*, laid down on 4 July 1965, designed as a dual-purpose ship, an Atlantic liner which was also a resort hotel able to follow the sun. A few weeks before *Queen Elizabeth II* went down the ways at John Brown's, the *Queen Mary* put out on her last voyage. It was a long one. While the Cunard directors were wondering what to do with the old liner at the end of her career, an offer reached them from out of the blue. Long Beach in California was willing to buy her for $3,400,000 (£1,736,666). The company accepted the bid; and on 18 August 1967 the magnificent old lady left Southampton on the beginning of a cruise that took her to Lisbon, Las Palmas and Rio de Janeiro, and then round the Horn in the wake of Francis Drake's *Golden Hind* to the shores of his New Albion. It seemed fitting that a ship which had borne thousands of Americans across the ocean should find her last home in the United States. At great expense Long Beach converted her into a museum, convention centre and hotel. Visitors troop on board in their thousands to see Cabin MB2 where the Queen slept as Princess Elizabeth and to pore over all sorts of relics from the crew's paybooks to the instructions for burial at sea. Some even go on board to be married.

In the year after her arrival at Long Beach an American group agreed to take over the old

Below left: The 27,645-ton Oceanic, *seen here off New York. She was built in 1965.*

Below right: In 1975 P & O announced that the Oronsay *had been sold for breaking up. She was constructed by Vickers-Armstrong in 1950 and entered the London–Australia service in May 1951. She opened the extended Pacific sailings to San Francisco and Vancouver in 1954.*

peace, the 29,000-ton *Andrea Doria*, proud flagship of the Italia Line, came to a sad end in her fourth year of service. On the night of 25 July 1956 she was heading for New York when the 11,000-ton Swedish-American *Stockholm* ran into her in fog 45 miles south east of Nantucket. Many of her 1,134 passengers were asleep at the time. At 10.09 the following morning she sank, coming to rest on her starboard side 225ft down. Fifty-four lives were lost. Afterwards much thought was given to raising the 697ft hull. Someone had the idea of filling it with ping-pong balls, and someone else suggested that the ship should be cut up into 3,000,000 pairs of souvenir cuff-links.

One of the best-liked liners on the North Atlantic from 1946 to the beginning of the

Queen Elizabeth as a floating hotel, resort ship and convention centre on the Delaware at Philadelphia. The leader of the project wrote to the magazine *Ships Monthly* expressing his pleasure in the project, but the scheme failed and the *Queen Elizabeth* passed to another group which planned to use her for the same purpose at Port Everglades in Florida. This scheme too came to nothing, and Port Everglades was left with a huge embarrassment on its hands until the Chinese shipping magnate, Mr C. Y. Tung, bought the liner in 1970 with the intention of converting her into a university cruise-ship which would be chartered to the United Nations Organization in the service of world fellowship. As *Seawise University* – a pun on his initials – she departed for Hong Kong; and there on 9 January 1972 she caught fire in the harbour and was completely gutted. After the firemen had poured water into her for a day and a night, she rolled

Above: Italia Line's Raffaello, 45,933 tons, constructed in 1965.

over, destroyed by 'a person or persons unknown'.

The glory was departing from the North Atlantic. Little of it remained by the seventies. Some liners had ended at the shipbreakers, in Taiwan or elsewhere; others were cruising or combining cruises with regular voyages. Those broken up included the *Mauretania*, the *Manhattan* and *Washington* of the United States Lines and the *Nieuw Amsterdam* of Holland-America.

None had such an unusual end as the *Ile de France* which some years before had been deliberately sunk in shallow water for a film, *The Last Voyage*, on her way to shipbreakers at Osaka. The *Pasteur* had gone to Chandris Lines as the *Regina Magna* and the *America* as the *Australis*, the largest single-class liner in service; the *Empress of Canada* belonged to Carnival Cruise Lines, a subsidiary of American International Travel Service Inc.; the *Independence*

Right: P & O's Canberra, *45,000 tons. At the time of her launching in March 1960 she was the largest ship to have been built in Britain since the* Queen Elizabeth. *She was designed for 2,250 passengers.*

Above far right: The France.

Below far right: The Oriana *(41,923 tons) at Pago-Pago in Samoa. In December 1960 this luxury liner entered the P & O-Orient Lines service between London, Australia, New Zealand and California. Note her bulbous bow.*

Below centre: Cunard's latest in 1976, the Countess.

Below: The Queen Mary *leaving Southampton.*

and *Constitution* of American Export Isbrandtsen Lines were with Atlantic Far East Lines, a subsidiary of the C. Y. Tung Group; and the *Rotterdam* was sailing under the flag of the Netherlands Antilles. In 1975 the *United States* was reported to be rusting away at Norfolk, Virginia, at a cost of $1 million a year.

While there were hopes that the *Michelangelo* and *Raffaello* of the Italia Line might be turned into hospital ships for cancer patients, a question mark still hovered above the graceful bows of the *France*. The decision of the French Government to withdraw her in October 1974 provoked her crew to stage a sit-in-at-sea; the astonishing scene was witnessed by trade unionists and rich Americans united in support of a luxury ship which had been costing the taxpayer huge sums. In 1972 she had circumnavigated the world in 88 days. Two ladies from Texas paid the equivalent of nearly £30,000 for four cabins.

In the mid-seventies the Red Flag seemed to to be taking the place of the Red Duster on the Atlantic passenger routes. Two impressive Soviet liners of 20,000 tons were sailing to North America three times a year from Tilbury on the Thames, with a call at Le Havre. It was announced early in 1976 that one of them, the *Alexander Pushkin*, would leave for Montreal on 9 May, 9 June and 29 September, and the other, the *Mikhail Lermontov*, for New York on 23 May, 15 September and 17 October. Poland also had a liner on the Atlantic run. The *Stefan Batory* sailed monthly from Gdynia

to Montreal *via* Rotterdam and London, returning by way of Southampton and Rotterdam. Once a year when the St Lawrence is frozen she ends her outward voyage at New York instead of Montreal. She was formerly the Holland-America *Maasdam*, built in 1952.

Among all the sea changes the last great Cunarder continued to create her own legend. Something of the twenties spirit lived again in the *QE2*. We do not know what Samuel Cunard would have thought of the nine bars and the 200 different cocktails, the casino with its roulette and blackjack, the Theatre Bar and the Q4 night club where passengers might dance the hours and the miles away; but we can be sure that Dickens, the celebrated passenger in the *Britannia* of 1840, would have enjoyed describing it all for another volume of *American Notes*. Perhaps he would have ended with the question: 'Does anyone ever notice the sea?'

Sailing on the Trade Winds

THROUGHOUT THE WAR of American Independence the captains and crews of British frigates often had occasion to curse (and sometimes, more privately, to admire) the U.S. light, fast colonial vessels which gave them the slip with a confident ease that bordered upon nonchalance. The schooners in particular were an amazement. Whatever influences had a part in their making, they struck British observers as entirely and remarkably American, designed to meet the special needs of the colonists. With their two masts raked towards the stern and their fore-and-aft rig and square topsails, they combined speed and simplicity: they could be sailed with small crews and they needed little upkeep. Their sailing qualities had commended them to the authorities before the war when several of them were used as armed coastguard vessels. The characteristics which gave them their exceptional speed were their sail plan and the fine, sharp lines of their hulls. Some of them were as fast as any vessels afloat.

Whatever their ancestors, their descendants were very well known. The 'Virginia-built' schooners of the late eighteenth century came to be described as 'Baltimore-built', and then, in the war of 1812, as 'Baltimore clippers'. They probably owed their new name to nothing more mysterious than the fact they they could 'clip along' or go 'at a good clip'. Like their ancestors in the earlier war, they constantly eluded the British and the Americans employed them as blockade runners and privateers. Unfortunately the speed which had served them admirably in war made them ideal for the slave trade. In the course of suppressing that evil traffic, the Royal Navy captured a number which it then used against the slavers. It also built some new vessels incorporating elements of the Baltimore design and altered older ones to embody these improvements as far as possible. William Symonds, the Secretary of the Navy, made a profitable study of the American hulls. But the Baltimore clippers were not, strictly speaking, true clippers in the sense now given to that word. The true clipper was yet to come.

Some have said that she arrived in 1832 as the *Ann McKim* of Baltimore, and others that she appeared in 1839 as the *Scottish Maid*, built by Alexander Hall and Sons of Aberdeen for the passenger trade between England and Scotland. Neither claim is justified: the first vessel known to us which qualifies for the distinction of true clipper in hull design and rig, and not in speed alone, was the *Rainbow*, built at New York in 1845 and reputed to be the fastest ship of her day – a tragically short day, as it happened, for in 1848 she was lost at sea with all hands.

When the Napoleonic Wars ended at last in 1815, American shipowners and merchants had to choose between deep-hulled vessels which could carry large cargoes at a moderate speed and the long, sharp, narrow vessels which had less room for cargo but a much better turn of speed. Not surprisingly in the light of their maritime history, they plumped for speed. To help them the Federal Government altered the rules of tonnage measurement on which port charges were based. The packet ships prospered because of their speed and were followed, as competition grew more acute, by the clippers, which crossed the ocean even faster.

Just before the mid century clipper-building received a tremendous fillip. On 24 January 1848 a young man building a sawmill at Coloma on the American River in the Sacramento Valley noticed bright yellow flecks in the tail race, or sluice. The flecks were gold. When the news became known, a great rush west began. There was as yet no railroad across the continent and no canal across the isthmus of Panama: the fortune hunter had to go by ship round Cape Horn unless he were prepared to attempt the slow and dangerous journey overland. Clipper after clipper put out for California. The demand kept the shipbuilders busy and at the same time improved the design: some of the clippers were

famous for their speed. At New York between 1850 and 1853 William H. Webb built the *Celestial* of 810 tons; the *Challenge* of 2,006 tons; the *Comet* of 1,836; the *Sword Fish* of 1,034 tons; and the *Young America* of 1,962.

At East Boston in 1850 Donald McKay, who had already made his name as a builder of packet ships, launched the 1,534-ton *Stag Hound*, his first clipper. He had contracted to build her in 60 days. The launching from his yard at the bottom of Border Street drew a crowd estimated at over 10,000 in December weather so cold that everyone feared the tallow on the slipway would freeze. Far from sticking, the *Stag Hound* moved so fast that the foreman just managed to smash his bottle of Medford rum on her forefoot, shouting 'Stag Hound – your name's Stag Hound!' and losing his hat. She had a long, sharp bow and a light elliptical stern and her greatest breadth was amidships. New York was as much

surprised as Boston when the ship arrived there. On 1 February 1851, in a strong westerly breeze, she left the Battery, to pass Sandy Hook at ten knots.

From Valparaiso, where she spent five days, she made a passage of 42 days to San Francisco. Her time at sea was 108 days and her best day's run was 358 nautical miles. Donald McKay had no need to worry about his future as a builder of clipper ships. The *Stag Hound* provided a bold and successful illustration of the theory put forward by his friend John Willis Griffiths, the designer of the *Rainbow*. 'This daring innovator', wrote Richard McKay, grandson of the master builder, 'proposed a model of a knifelike, concave entrance, melting into an easy run to the midship section, where, instead of forward, he located the extreme breadth of beam. Thence this fullness of breadth melted again into the after end in lines almost as fine as those forward. In place of the codfish underbody, he gave his innovation a dead rise amidships.' Richard McKay added: 'The superior excellence of our ships was obtained wholly by the use of the waterline model in the designing of them!'

Such was the formula of McKay ships to come. Soon after the *Stag Hound* proved herself, Georges Frances Train, a famous Boston Ship-owner, told her creator that he wanted a vessel of 2,000 tons.

broken – by Donald McKay. In the *Sovereign of the Seas*, he produced a ship of 2,420 tons which outsailed the *Flying Cloud*. She measured 265ft in extreme length and 44ft in beam. Her mainmast rose 92ft 9in. and her bowsprit, of hard pine, extended 20ft outboard and was 34in. in diameter. As no merchant in New England would buy such a vessel, McKay ran her himself with his brother Lauchlan in command. She left for San Francisco loaded with 2,950 tons of

Later the *Boston Daily Atlas* reported: 'If great length, sharpness of ends, with proportionate breadth and depth, conduce to speed, the *Flying Cloud* must be uncommonly swift, for in all these she is great. Her length on the keel is 208ft, on deck 225, and over all, from the knight heads to the taffrail, 235 – extreme breadth of beam 41ft, depth of hold 21½, including 7 feet 8 inches height of between-decks, dead-rise at half floor 20 inches, rounding of sides 6 inches, and sheer about 3ft.'

On 3 June 1851, in a westerly breeze which soon freshened to a gale, she ran past Sandy Hook under three skysails, royals, topgallant, to topmast and square lower studding sails. Her destination was California, and she swept through the Golden Gate at 11.30 on the morning of 30 August, having made the passage in the record time of 89 days 21 hours from Sandy Hook. However McKay records were made to be

merchandise, the largest cargo ever despatched from the port of New York and arrived at the Golden Gate in 103 days. It was said that she had beaten every vessel that sailed within a month of her. She certainly beat the steamship *Canada* across the Atlantic. The *Canada* put in at Liverpool to be greeted by a large canvas sign telling all on board that the *Sovereign of the Seas* had already arrived, in 13 days 22 hours.

Thanks to the master builder from Nova

Above: The three-masted barque Rapido, *built at the little Cumberland port of Harrington (now part of Workington) in 1855.*

Left: Among the ships well-known at Hong Kong in the last great era of sail was the 814-ton Maiden Queen, *shown here in a painting of 1860.*

Scotia, Americans in the Far West no longer felt on the other side of the world. Triumph followed triumph until McKay built his masterpiece, the *Great Republic* of 1853. After she had been destroyed by fire – the lurid doom to which his clippers seemed fated – he designed the *Lightning* (burnt at Geelong, Melbourne, in October 1869) for James Baines of the Liverpool Black Ball Line. The *Argus* said of her maiden voyage: 'Not a ripple curled before her cutwater, nor did the water break at a single place along her sides. She left a wake straight as an arrow, and this was the only mark of her progress.'

At two o'clock on Saturday afternoon, 18 February 1854, this splendid ship left Boston for Liverpool. Her log for 1 March reads:

> Wind S., strong gales; bore away for the North Channel, carried away the foretopsail and lost jib; hove the log several times, and found the ship going through the water at the rate of 18 to 18½ knots per hour: lee rail under water, and the rigging slack, saw the Irish land at 9.30 pm. Distance run in the twenty-four hours, 436 miles.

This record for a day's run by a sailing vessel still holds. About 30 years passed before it was exceeded by a steamship.

In 1851, soon after the discovery of gold in Australia, James Baines entered the Australian trade with the record-breaking *Marco Polo*. Encouraged by her success, he had then chartered the *Sovereign of the Seas* at Liverpool. The clipper sailed for Melbourne with a cargo valued at a million dollars and arrived in 77 days, hence his order for the *Lightning*. The Australian gold rush, like the wilder dash to California, brought a sudden demand for fast vessels. After landing their passengers, cargo, and mails, they sailed home with gold and wool; the *Sovereign of the Seas* carried more than four tons of gold from Melbourne to London in January 1854.

James Baines ordered three more clippers from the same builder: the *Champion of the Seas,* the *James Baines* and the *Donald McKay*. The first two were admired by Queen Victoria when they were taking troops on board at Portsmouth in 1857. All served on the Australian run and they made a celebrated quartet. Bets were laid on their passage times and their arrivals were announced in the Exchanges in Liverpool and London.

With the end of the gold rush, the outward trade slackened. But the clippers still had work to do. For some years past they had also sailed to the Far East. The monopoly of the China trade long enjoyed by the British East India Company had ended in 1849, and in the same year Britain had abandoned the old Navigation Acts requiring imports to be carried in British vessels, or vessels of the country where the goods had been produced. At once the clippers began to compete with one another in fetching tea from the Orient. Some of them had already carried it to New York; the *Stag Hound*, after her first San Francisco run, returned home by way of Canton with a cargo which was sold by auction.

Hitherto the tea drunk in Britain had been a year old. At the time that it was ready for shipment, in June and July, the south-west monsoon was blowing in the China Sea, making it hard for ships to pass through the Sunda Straits. As fast vessels which could beat to windward, the clippers met this difficulty and satisfied a demand which they also helped to create. The announcement that a ship had put in with the 'new teas' convinced the public that greater freshness meant much better flavour. Yet the tea-drinking British were depending for their cargoes on vessels built by the Americans, to whom they had once tried to sell an enormous surplus, some of which ended in the cold water of Boston harbour. Under the tonnage measurement rules, a clipper registered in Britain had a much greater tonnage than her American-registered counterpart and therefore had to pay much higher taxation and port charges. At length, with the introduction of a new rule, British and Continental shipowners had a chance of competing on better terms, no longer penalized for the overall length of their craft.

The first true clippers which were also truly British came from Alexander Hall and Sons in Aberdeen. James and William Hall of that company had carried out experiments with models in a glass-sided tank containing water on which red-coloured turpentine was poured. When a

model was drawn across the water, the movement of the coloured fluid revealed the effect of different hull and bow forms. In 1839 the Halls built the schooner *Scottish Maid*, which has been claimed as the first clipper because of her speed. The company had its first true clipper, the *Stornoway*, in 1850. She was a small vessel of 595 tons, 157.8ft long with a beam of 18.5ft. Her immediate successor, the *Chrysolite*, was a similar craft launched in 1853. Both clippers served in the China trade, the *Stornoway* maintaining her Far East runs for nearly fifteen years.

The Aberdeen Company was only a little ahead of R. and H. Green, the Thames builders renowned for their Blackwall frigates. Their *Challenger* of 1852, a bigger and faster clipper than the Scottish vessels, made an outward passage to China in 101 days.

By the mid 1850s shipbuilders in various parts of Britain were following the Aberdeen lead, including Rennie, Johnson and Rankin of Liverpool who laid down the *Fiery Cross* which was four times winner of the extra premium paid to the first ship docking at London with new teas. Aberdeen had already turned out the *Cairngorm*, which gave excellent service to Jardine, Matheson and Company, and the *Vision*. The *Robin Hood* was ready in 1856. All had the plain Aberdeen

clipper bow and were full-rigged, with four or five yards on each mast and studding sails or stunsails to increase the driving power.

American clippers were larger than the British ships but their size did not guarantee them a better speed, especially in the tricky and dangerous China Sea. As their hulls were of wood, their construction had to be massive. They were, indeed, too large for the loading arrangements at ports in China; smaller vessels could be filled

Below far left: The True Briton.

Above left: At anchor in the Mersey, the Eagle *(1,020 tons) prepares to sail. The lithograph is from a painting by Thomas Dove.*

Below: The Golden Light *ablaze.*

more quickly. Wooden ships in the China trade were copper-sheathed until 'composite construction' came to be used from about 1863. Inspired by the iron ships on the Australian run, shipbuilders gave their tea clippers interior frameworks of iron and then planked the hull with wood, to which a sheathing of copper or yellow metal was added below the waterline. Between 1839 and 1860 the British Patent Office received more than thirty applications relating to composite construction.

The British clippers were helped by ill-winds in the United States, the depression of 1857 and then the Civil War from 1861 to 1865. American shipbuilding declined, and the British tea-trade prospered in answer to an increasing demand. Every year at the end of May the Pagoda Anchorage at Foochow was a forest of tall masts. The era of the great tea-races had begun.

One day in 1865 the *Fiery Cross* and the *Serica* put out from Foochow at the same time, bound for London. After taking separate courses on entering the China Sea, they kept sighting each other. In the English Channel they broke out their signal flags together off St Catherine's

Above: The Harbinger.

Above right: The Bosphorus, *owned by Rathbone Brothers of Liverpool.*

Below right: The Carlisle Castle.

Point, and off Beachy Head they were neck and neck. Then, off Deal, the *Serica* picked up her tug two miles ahead of the *Fiery Cross*. She looked the probable winner, but her rival, brought into London Docks by a more powerful tug, was a tide ahead of her at the end. The two clippers had completed the passage in 107 days.

The most famous of the races took place in 1866 after the *Fiery Cross*, *Ariel*, *Serica*, *Taeping* and *Taitsing* had sailed from Foochow in that order. They all put out within the space of 30 hours, leaving behind four other clippers which had not yet finished loading. The *Fiery Cross* reached Anjer in 20 days, one day ahead of her rivals, and then her lead grew less as all five sped

before the trade winds of the Indian Ocean, running down to the Cape of Good Hope. They sailed by Flores in the Azores, where the *Revenge* had fought her last battle, on the same day. For the greater part of Sunday, 5 September, the *Ariel* and *Taeping* were in sight of each other as they headed up the Channel at fourteen knots. The *Ariel* signalled her number off Deal at eight o'clock on the Monday morning and the *Taeping* followed suit in ten minutes. Later that day both of them reached London, where the *Serica* also arrived, shortly before the dock gates closed. The *Taeping* was in the London Docks at 9.45 pm, the *Ariel* in the East India Docks at 10.15, and the *Serica* in the West Indies Docks

at 11.30. They had crossed 16,000 miles of sea in 99 days. The *Fiery Cross* and *Taitsing* put in two days later. Also rans though they were, they had nevertheless beaten the previous record by six days.

The *Taeping*, *Ariel*, *Sir Lancelot*, *Titania*, *Lahloo* and *Kaisow*, all built by Robert Steele and Sons, made some of the fastest passages ever recorded on the China run. In 1866–7 the *Ariel* was only 80 days, between pilots, from London to Hong Kong; in 1869 the *Sir Lancelot* passed the Lizard 84 days after leaving Foochow; and in 1871 the *Titania* completed the passage in 93 days.

In 1868 the magnificent *Thermopylae*, built

by Hood of Aberdeen, went down the ways. Her maiden voyage took her from London to Melbourne in 60 days. On the passage to China she was only 28 days from Newcastle in New South Wales to Shanghai, by way of the Sunda Straits. At another time, she sailed from Sydney to the Horn in seventeen days when other fast vessels were pleased to cover the same distance in 21.

She was painted Aberdeen green with white lower masts, yardarms, bowsprit and blocks. Her figurehead, also white, represented Leonidas, king of Sparta, the hero who stood against the invading Persians in the pass at Thermopylae. She was an out-and-out clipper. Although she is always linked with her great rival, the *Cutty Sark*, neither vessel ever won the tea race from China. The nearest they came to winning it was on their way home from Shanghai in 1872. They both left on 21 July. Two days out, after they had been delayed by fog, the fore topgallant sail of the *Cutty Sark* split in a gale. All down the China Sea they were in sight of each other, one leading and then the other. The *Thermopylae* was a little ahead at Anjer, but a few days later the *Cutty Sark* had the advantage in a spell of strong breezes – the weather which suited her best. But in latitude 34 degrees South a strong westerly gale, after splitting a number of her sails, carried away the rudder and with it her chance of victory.

The two ships had been built when the tea trade was nearly at an end. With the opening of the Suez Canal in 1870, the tea clipper yielded to the steamship. Ships like the *Cutty Sark* and *Thermopylae* turned to the Australian wool trade, but it was not long before these opportunities ended as well. The beautiful old clippers had to be content with whatever work they could find.

In 1889 the *Thermopylae* was bought by Robert Reford of Montreal, who sent her from Cardiff to Singapore with a cargo of coal. Afterwards she traded across the Pacific from Victoria in British Columbia, carrying lumber on her outward voyages and bringing back rice and other cereals. Her sail plan had been twice reduced in the Australian trade, and now she was converted to barque rig, with her topmasts shortened by six feet. She could be sailed by a crew of 32.

The *Thermopylae* ended her days in the Portuguese Navy as a coaling hulk. Her last hours did much to compensate for this indignity: in 1909, before the Queen of Portugal, she was taken to sea during a regatta and sunk by a British Whitehead torpedo. She went down in flames.

Towards the close of the great age of sail Victoria had a number of fine old ships, among them Heap's *Antiope*, formerly a wool clipper, and the graceful little *Titania* which belied her age and pleased the Hudson Bay Company by daring the stormy westerlies on the London–Victoria run and arriving in 90 to 100 days.

Of Donald McKay's 33 clippers at least nine were accidentally burned: the *Stag Hound* off

Above left: Charles Lamport built the fast clipper Scawfell *of wood at Workington in 1858. She could carry 1,020,000lb of tea. From Rathbone Bros of Liverpool she passed in 1872 to Wilson and Blain of South Shields, and then in 1880 to Hutchinson of Newcastle. On 9 January 1883 she was abandoned at 47 deg 30 min N, 11 deg 10 min W with seven feet of water in the hold and her pumps choked with coal from her cargo.*

Above right: The American clipper Comet. *In 1854 she sailed from Liverpool to Hong Kong in 83 days 21 hours (17 June to 7 September) between pilots, or 86 days 16 hours anchor to anchor.*

Following pages: The barque Sindia, *a water colour of 1887 by R.H. Neville-Cumming. She was a steel ship on the Calcutta run. In 1901 she was wrecked off Ocean City, New Jersey.*

Pernambuco; the *Flying Cloud* near St John; *New Brunswick* while she was being repaired; the *Westward Ho!* in harbour at Callao; the *Empress of the Seas* at Queenscliff (Port Phillip); the *Great Republic* (sold and rebuilt) at Peck Slip, New York; the *Lightning* at Geelong (Australia); the *Commodore Perry* near Bombay; the *Mastiff* at sea, two days out from San Francisco. The *Glory of the Seas* was set on fire deliberately for her metal at Endolyne Beach on Puget Sound in May 1923.

The best fate of all befell the *Cutty Sark*. She was built at Dumbarton in Scotland by two young men, William Dundas Scott-Moncrieff, a civil engineer, and Hercules Linton, a naval architect. Captain John Willis wanted a ship that would beat the *Thermopylae*, recently landed at Aberdeen. The clipper which the two partners provided for him had a length of 212ft, a beam of 36ft, a depth of 21ft and a gross tonnage of 963. They had agreed to build her for £16,150, or about £17 a ton, but this charge, although it was not especially low for the 1860s, failed to meet the cost and the partners went into voluntary liquidation.

The *Cutty Sark* left the Woodyard at Dumbarton on 22 November 1869 and began her maiden voyage on 16 February 1870, leaving London for Shanghai. She was not long in the tea trade, and it was on the Australian run that she gave of her finest. Besides holding the best average, 73¾ days, for the years from 1874 to 1880, she made some astonishing daily runs in

the Forties. On one day she logged 363 miles. There was a time, too, when she raced the P & O mail steamer *Britannia* from Cape Gabo to Sydney.

A time came when she could no longer be made to pay, despite her fine performance under Captain Richard Woodget. In 1895, John Willis sold her to some Lisbon brothers who renamed her the *Ferreira* and kept her for over 20 years. After she had been dismasted off the Cape of Good Hope in 1916, she was towed into Table Bay and re-rigged as a barquentine.

On a rough day in 1922 she took refuge at Falmouth where she was recognized by Captain Wilfred Dowman, who had once been passed by her at sea. Buying her back from the Portuguese, he restored her clipper rig and used her as a boys' training ship until his death in 1937. She was then given to the Incorporated Thames Nautical Training College. In 1938 she was towed from Falmouth to Greenhithe on the Thames. There she remained, surviving the wartime bombs. When the college had no further need of her, she was offered to the National Maritime Museum at Greenwich and a preservation society was formed on the initiative of Prince Philip and Frank Carr. The task began of restoring her as a China tea clipper of the 1870s. In June 1957 Queen Elizabeth declared her open to the public – to the hundreds of thousands of people, both young and old, who would be welcomed on board her in her dry dock at Greenwich.

SINDIA

H Neville Cumming.
1885.

Cargo and Container Ships

DURING THE MIDDLE AGES the English ranged the seas of Europe. They carried wool to France and cloth to the Low Countries; they passed through the Straits of Gibraltar, between the Pillars of Hercules which once had marked the limits of the known world; they sailed to Venice and the Greek islands and called at the busy ports of the Levant, sometimes on voyages lasting a year.

Not until the reign of Elizabeth did the English devote any serious thought to making a settlement in the New World. Most voyagers – the Pilgrim Fathers were among the great exceptions – intended to come back again bringing something with them unless they were looking, like Cabot, for the way to richer cargoes. Men dreamed of finding the North-West Passage or – somewhere near Mozambique perhaps – the mysterious Land of Prester John.

Valuable cargoes were indeed brought home from afar. On 31 December 1600 the British East India Company came into existence, and traded until 1 June 1874. In the course of that long period, two and three-quarter centuries, it became a vast trading empire with powers resembling those of a sovereign state – for 'John Company' had its own army and navy, civil service and mercantile marine, and even a college (Haileybury in Hertfordshire). It was formed by London merchants who had petitioned the Queen for a charter granting them the monopoly of the trade. Before they had received this document, they bought four vessels, the *Dragon* (formerly a privateer), and the *Hector*, *Ascension* and *Susan*. Accompanied by a supply ship, the *Guest*, the four left the Thames in February 1600 carrying trade goods together with presents for the Indian princes. Calm weather in the Channel delayed them, and it was April when they put out from Dartmouth. They reached the Canary Islands in May, crossed the Equator in June and were then held back by more calms. When they came to the site

of Cape Town in September all on board were suffering from scurvy except those who had been given three spoonsful of lemon juice every morning. They voyaged for a little more than a year before anchoring off Sumatra where they were welcomed by a royal procession of elephants.

Marco Polo had evidently told the truth. But what the English most needed from the wealth of the Indies was pepper. They filled their holds with it in the islands and then set out for England. They had been away nearly three years, and when they returned after many trials and tragedies the Queen was dead, London was stricken by the plague and the market already had more pepper than the public needed for a time. However the voyage eventually brought in a large profit.

At first the East India Company was concerned with the spices of the islands off the south-eastern corner of Asia. It showed little interest in India itself until the Dutch, who had had their own East India Company since 1602, fought them successfully for the Spice Islands trade and compelled them to find other cargoes on the Indian subcontinent. The new venture had immense consequences, the creation of Britain's Indian Empire.

After leasing the Deptford yard for 20 years, John Company decided that it would be less costly to hire ships. Nearly all the later East Indiamen came from the yard at Blackwall, where a whole community derived its livelihood from shipbuilding and seafaring. The vessels looked very much like the warships of their time and were sometimes mistaken for them. At night they snugged down; unlike the clippers which succeeded them, they had no need to hurry. Life on board was comfortable by the standards of the time within a stern naval-style discipline and the company took care of its men at sea and on shore. One of its many rules laid down the complement to be carried; 101 for a ship of 750 to 800 tons, 110 for one of 900 tons, and so on.

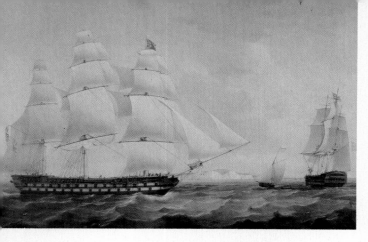

Among the commodities found in the hold of a homeward-bound Indiaman there might be black and green tea, pepper, nutmegs, green ginger, coffee, sugar, rice, sago, silk, cotton, hemp, chinaware, camphor, cochineal, gum arabic, coral, shellac, aloes, buffalo hides, cowries, saltpetre, sandalwood, redwood, spikenard, elephants' teeth, myrrh and opium. By late 1621 the Company had sent out woollen goods, iron, tin, lead and other commodities valued altogether at £319,211 and had imported from the East cargoes bought there for £375,288 and sold in England for £2,044,600.

After the Company had lost its monopoly, the great East Indiamen were replaced by the so-called Blackwall frigates, merchantmen which owed the first part of their name to their place of origin, the Thames yard of Green and Wigram, and the second part to their appearance. They varied in size from 800 tons to 1,000 or 1,200. As fast vessels, they had a better chance than the conventional Indiaman of competing with the steamships. Naval strictness obtained on board.

By the end of the eighteenth century two other vessels were beginning to attract attention: the barque, square-rigged on the fore and main and fore-and-aft rigged on the mizzen, and the barquentine, square-rigged on the foremast only, the main and mizzen having the fore-and-aft arrangement. The big barques competed with the steamers towards the end of the great age of sail. They earned their living on the longer passages, rounding the Horn in waters too rough for the steamships. They took coal, grain and steel rails to Chile and Peru, bringing back nitrates and hides. Most of them were of 2,000

or 2,500 tons. The *France I*, a five-master of 3,784 tons built at Glasgow in 1890 for A. D. Bordes, could claim to be the largest sailing vessel in the world at the time of her launching. When the Panama Canal provided a steamship route to Chile and Peru, the great barques vanished from the trade routes, some of them to be rescued and preserved. In 1973 the South Street Seaport Museum, New York had the hull of the four-masted barque *Moshulu* towed across the Atlantic from Amsterdam.

One early steamship which braved the far seas was Brunel's *Great Britain*, floated off at Bristol in the presence of the Prince Consort

Page 94: The P & O cargo-vessel Strathalvie.

Far left: An East Indiaman.

Left: The steel barque Bermuda, *built by Russell of Port Glasgow in 1893.*

defeated. When they began to fade from the seas with the opening of the Suez Canal, ship owner Alfred Holt had fresh competition to face from other companies using the waterway, but his company survived and flourished. In the Second World War more than 40 of its ships, over half the fleet, were sunk, but these appalling losses did not prevent it from recovering its place as the leading freight carrier between Europe and the Far East. The Holt flag still flies, on vessels

on 19 July 1843 as the largest vessel in the world – 322ft in length, 50ft 6in. in beam with a gross tonnage of 3,270 – and the first ocean-going ship to have an iron hull and a screw propeller. About 20,000 people paid 25c each to go on board her when she first arrived at New York. But on her fifth crossing she ran ashore in Dundrum Bay within sight of the Mountains of Mourne and the cost of repairing her after she had been stranded for eleven months proved too much for her owners, the Great Western Steamship Company. She was taken over and put into the Australian trade. After making another passage to the United States in 1852, she left for Melbourne with a cargo which included gold and silver worth about £1 million.

At the end of her thirty-second Melbourne voyage, she was laid up for six years before Antony Gibbs, Sons and Company bought her in 1882, removed her engines, and ran her as a three-master. She completed two passages from Liverpool to San Francisco, coal out and wheat home, and was on her way with another cargo of coal when she encountered a gale off the Horn. In the Falklands, where she put in for repairs, she was found to be a 'constructive total loss'. From 1886 to 1933 she served the Falkland Islands Company as a hulk for the storage of wool and coal and then, after part of her decking had been used for a bridge over the Fitzroy River and a jetty at Port Stanley, she was towed to Sparrow Cove and abandoned. There she remained until a group of enthusiasts rescued her in 1970. With church bells ringing, she was towed on a pontoon into Port Stanley, to begin her long voyage home. At the end of six and a half weeks and 7,600 miles, she arrived home at Bristol and entered the drydock with Prince Philip on board. Although the work of restoring her would obviously take years, she immediately became a great attraction in that ancient port.

During the period of her service on the Australian run she was challenged on the China route by three ten-knot ships, the *Agamemnon*, *Ajax* and *Achilles*. The *Agamemnon* put out for China on 19 April 1866. She was the first of the Ocean Steam Ship Company's Blue Funnel vessels, a series identified by names taken from the *Iliad* and the *Odyssey*. Sailing by way of the Cape, the three sisters gave an excellent account of themselves. But the clippers were not quickly

Below left: The Hon East India Company's Inglis *leaving St Helena in July 1830 with other ships.*

Top right: The 3,765 ton barque Brilliant. *In 1901 she and her sister ship* Daylight *ranked as the largest wind jammers under the British flag and the largest four-masters afloat.*

Above right: 'Deptford Dockyard' by C. B. Scott.

now administered by Ocean Transport and Trading.

No shipping concern suffered more directly from the opening of the Suez Canal than the Peninsular and Oriental Steam Navigation Company. Hitherto it had maintained two large fleets, one for European waters and the other for the tropics, with special river steamers, horse-drawn carriages and comfortable stopping places linking them on the overland route. The whole system was suddenly obsolete. P & O met the challenge by drawing a new revenue from cargo transport instead of relying entirely on passenger fares, mail contracts and small select cargoes.

Below left : Indiamen in China Seas, by W.J. Huggins. The artist was born in 1781, served at sea with the East India Company, and in 1834 was appointed marine painter to King William IV.

Below right : The sailing-barge May at Cowes.

Above right : A collier brig.

When it celebrated the Golden Jubilee of Queen Victoria by ordering the 6,000-ton *Victoria, Britannia, Oceania* and *Arcadia*, it had the satisfaction of knowing that since the completion of the canal the size of its fleet had grown from 80,000 tons to 200,000. It was later to embrace company after company: among them the British Steam Navigation Company in 1914, and the General Steam Navigation Company in 1920.

Like the P & O in Egypt, the Royal Mail Steam Packet Company had an overland route, across the Isthmus of Panama; it was opened in 1846 before a railway was built. Royal Mail became famous for those 'great steamers white and gold' rolling down to Rio as in Kipling's poem. Not the least interesting of its other activities, notably in the Australian trade and the Far East, were the small steamers which it introduced in the area of the Windward Islands and Jamaica, calling at little bays and creeks for cargoes of fruit, cocoa and sugar and carrying them to Bridgetown, Barbados or Port of Spain where they were transferred to the mainline mail or cargo ship.

The Union-Castle Line possessed, besides its fast mail steamers, a fleet of intermediate vessels of large cargo capacity designed to steam at a moderate speed on a very low coal consumption. In the 1970s the Union-Castle Mail Steamship Company, in association with the South African Marine Corporation would still be running a passenger and cargo service to Cape ports.

While the big ships sailed the oceans, innumerable smaller craft moved in and out of every

Above: Square-riggers and other ships from many nations met in London River for the Festival of Sail in the summer of 1975. Behind the sailing barges in this picture is the three-masted Russian barque Tovarisch.

harbour and along every navigable river. The Chinese and Japanese had their junks, the Arabs their dhows, the Spanish their feluccas, the Americans their fast schooners: there was no end to the variety. In Britain a descendant of the Viking longship, the Humber keel, carried general cargoes on its own river and also on the Yorkshire Ouse. Along the East Coast, wherries and hoys passed each other and the collier brigs went by, sailing humbly between the north-east

ports and London but stout enough to reach the south of the world and come back again.

Where nothing else could float, the Thames spritsail barges sailed. These craft with their red, brown and buff sails would carry any legitimate cargo from coke to cattle cake. A 'stackie' would call at a country farm, take on hay, and sail away like a floating rick with one of the crew sitting on the top and calling instructions to the other. Britain owed much to its small craft. The trading

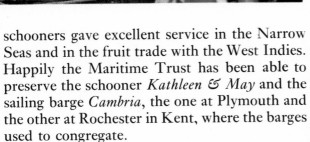

schooners gave excellent service in the Narrow Seas and in the fruit trade with the West Indies. Happily the Maritime Trust has been able to preserve the schooner *Kathleen & May* and the sailing barge *Cambria,* the one at Plymouth and the other at Rochester in Kent, where the barges used to congregate.

All sorts of vessels came out of Bideford and Appledore in Devon; brigs, brigantines, barquentines, topsail schooners, ketches, smacks,

Previous pages: The 300-ton topsail schooner Sir Winston Churchill *of Britain's Sail Training Association.*

Near right: The stately Libertad *of the Argentinian Navy.*

Far right: Italy's Amerigo Vespucci, *another ship which brings the old romance of sail to modern naval training. She was launched at Naples in February 1931 and modernized in 1951 and 1958. Her sail area is 22,600 square feet.*

sloops and polackers. According to the *Universal Register* in 1749, Bideford 'frequently sent out fifty sail of ships to the Newfoundland Fishery, and others were sent to Liverpool and Warrington to fetch rock salt which was here dissolved by the sea water into brine and then boiled up into a 'new salt' with which they cured their herrings and cod'. This river port kept its old tryst with Virginia where Grenville had taken the first English colonists, his flagship a vessel contributed by the Virgin Queen herself. In the first half of the eighteenth century Bideford merchants 'imported in their own ships more tobacco than any other port in England, except London'. The cargoes were stored in the Colonial Buildings, warehouses at East-the-Water.

In the course of the nineteenth century most of the work done by such craft as brigs and schooners was taken over by steam vessels. The collier brig, which had replaced the collier bark early in the century, was itself replaced by a vessel using the same sort of fuel that it carried. In 1852 Charles Palmer's *John Bowes*, an iron-screw collier, took on her first cargo at Sunder-land and disposed of it at Blackwall within 48 hours. She could carry about 540 tons, twice as much as the average collier brig.

Coal for ports outside Britain was often carried by tramp steamer. Of all the vessels in the British merchant fleet, none has been more useful than the adventurous tramp. She may be called a 'general-purpose ship' now, but her old name is an honourable one, deriving from the unscheduled character of her voyages and not from her appearance. The three-island tramp came into demand near the beginning of this century. When the export of coal from Britain declined, owners sent their vessels out to look for cargoes in other countries, coal and grain being the commonest before the First World War. Few of the vessels were of more than 10,000 tons deadweight.

Confronted with hundreds of companies over a long period – on the Great Lakes and the St Lawrence alone at the beginning of the century more than 50 steamer lines were operating – we can do no more than note the huge variety of vessels, cargoes and routes. Taken together they

Above left: One of OCL's container-ships in the Europe–Australia trade is the Moreton Bay *(29,100 tons deadweight), launched on 22 August 1968.*

Centre left: A roll-on, roll-off vessel.

Below left: A LASH freighter.

Near right: The tanker Esso Minden.

Far right: The tanker Esso Demetia, *built in 1973 with a gross tonnage of 125,293.*

may remind us of the contrast which one of Masefield's poems draws, between the quinquereme of Nineveh, the stately Spanish galleon and the third ship in his procession:

> Dirty British coaster with a salt-caked smoke stack
> Butting through the Channel in the mad March days,
> With a cargo of Tyne coal,
> Road-rail, pig-lead,
> Firewood, iron-ware, and cheap tin trays.

The variety of cargoes found vivid illustration in the warehouses at the London docks. There one might have seen great quantities of wool, brought by ship to the island which once supplied the wool markets of Europe; wine in casks, butts and pipes; carpets from far-off deserts; rows of elephant tusks and rhinoceros horns; pieces of jade; cases of shredded codfish; cowhides packed with sarsaparilla; iron bottles holding quicksilver. Behind drab walls one came upon the spices of the Orient and the perfumes of Arabia. The old romance of the sea could be found in the warehouses of London's dockland.

Nowadays all is different in the Pool of London. The East India Docks closed in 1967; the St Katherine in 1968; the London in 1969; and the Surrey Commercial in 1970. But downriver at Tilbury facilities for new methods of sea transport had made London the second container port in Europe. The 'container revolution' had arrived, and the Port of London Authority was ready for it.

the ship. All the long, awkward and expensive business of conventional handling is therefore eliminated with a corresponding saving in time, and the cargo can be handled at about twice the speed of the traditional break-bulk, reducing the cargo liner's stay in port by two-thirds. Tremendous capital investment is required, however, before these advantages can be enjoyed.

Immediately after the Second World War shipowners concentrated on the straightforward task of repairing their losses and making themselves ready for normal business again. The great changes did not begin for another decade. They were pioneered by Seatrain Lines of New York which, as early as 1929, had opened a service between New York, Houston and Havana carrying freight cars in cradles on board special ships. Their first vessel, before they turned to the Sun Shipbuilding Corporation of Chester, Pennsylvania, was constructed on the Tyne by Swan, Hunter and Wigham Richardson. They entered the deep-sea container business in 1959.

For a time many European shipowners were unconvinced that the idea would succeed and were reluctant to adopt a course that would make their existing fleets out-of-date. They were also scared of the cost. Eventually a number of companies formed three international consortia, the Atlantic Container Line (North Atlantic trade), Associated Container Transportation Limited (Australasian trade) and Overseas Containers Limited (also Australasian). They are called rather confusingly by their initials. The Overseas Containers group (OCL) was formed by P & O, the British and Commonwealth Shipping Company, Furness Withy and Company, and the Ocean Steam Ship Company; Associated Container Transportation (ACT) by Ben Line, Blue Star Line, Cunard, Ellerman Lines and T. and J. Harrison.

Another system involving the use of pallets was pioneered in London by the Fred. Olsen Lines running from Millwall Dock to Scandinavia, the Mediterranean and North America. The cargo is moved on and off through doors in the sides of the vessel, and this horizontal method of handling makes for speed.

There were more changes to come. A company at New Orleans devised the system known as LASH, from Lighter Aboard Ship. The name more or less explains the idea. A LASH vessel takes on specially-designed lighters, and sometimes standard containers, using her own gantry crane. The lighters are themselves the transport at the terminal. They can be taken along inland waterways if the draught permits.

The first LASH freighter, the *Acadia Forest* built by Uraga Heavy Industries of Yousuka, Japan in 1969, was designed to carry 73 lighters, each of 370 tons capacity, handled by a 510-ton travelling crane on rails. She was registered at Christiansand, Norway, chartered to the Central

Above: Unloading sugar.

Below: The Greek bulk carrier Pythia *seen off Long Beach, California. Built in Japan in 1972, she transports dry bulk cargoes such as coal and grain.*

Right: Loading a container-ship at Bremerhaven in Germany.

There is nothing mysterious about the containers. The unattractive word 'containerization' suggests some highly complex process involving electronics, but the principle employed is quite simple and not even very modern. Britain's railways introduced it for road and rail many years ago. The containers are metal boxes usually up to 40ft in length with an 8ft-square cross section. They differ from the railway boxes in that they are designed for road, rail and sea and are of a standard pattern which allows them to be used internationally. They are pre-packed by the company shipping the goods or at the container depots, and are not unpacked until they reach the customer or the container depot nearest to him. Loading is controlled by a computer which decides the position of each container in

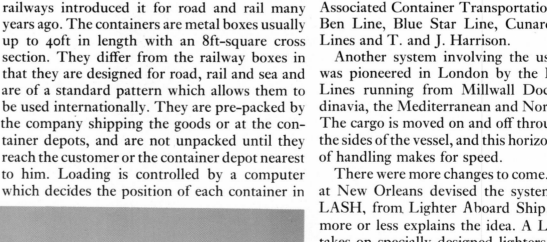

Right : The coaster
Victress *with a Thames lighter.*

Far right : Evening on the waterfront.

Below : The collier
Ben Ain *at Douglas, capital of the Isle of Man.*

Below far right : The P & O oil/bulk/ore carrier Kildare *(83,714 tons), built in 1972.*

Above: Loading cattle at Madagascar.

Right: The deck of a 110,000-ton bulk-carrier at Port Talbot in South Wales.

Gulf Steamship Corporation, and put into service between United States Gulf ports, the Thames and Rotterdam. Her tonnage was given as 43,000 deadweight. The size of an ultra-modern vessel is usually expressed in terms of deadweight (dwt), the total weight of the cargo, stores and fuel which she carries at her maximum permitted draught, as distinct from gross tonnage, total internal volume of the ship.

In 1972 the Lykes Bros Steamship Company of New Orleans introduced the first Seabee ship, the *Doctor Lykes* (20,500 gross tons) delivered by the General Dynamics Corporation of Quincy, Massachusetts. A Seabee vessel carries 38 barges. They are placed on board two at a time through a stern elevator. Tugs position them over a submerged platform which is then raised to the required level for a transporter to shift them into the storage area.

Yet another development is the extension to cargo vessels of the roll-on, roll-off system used for the conveyance of cars and trucks in passenger ferries. With roll-on, roll-off freight, the road vehicle drives on to the ship, load and all, and drives off again at its destination, the load having remained in place throughout the voyage. Besides saving much time, the method reduces the risk of damage and theft.

The most conspicuous vessel of all on the seas today is the giant tanker. In 1968 the Blandford Shipping Company of London took delivery of the largest vessel ever to trade under the British flag. She was the 210,822-dwt steam-turbine

tanker *Bulford* built by Sasebo Heavy Industries of Japan. A few years later the biggest vessels under the British flag were two more tankers, the *Globtik Tokyo* and the *Globtik London* constructed by Ishikawajima-Harima Heavy Industries of Kure. They were both of 477,000 dwt. Similarly, the 250,262-dwt tanker *Esso Hibernia* from Swan Hunter was the biggest ship ever built in Britain until Scott-Lithgow produced the 268,235-dwt tanker *Nordic Clansman* for the Anglo-Norness Group. Everyone guessed that something even larger would soon appear.

In 1975 the world had more tankers than it needed. Orders for large oil-carriers were cancelled almost daily and a huge tonnage lay idle. Japanese shipyards, having specialized in the

Top: Baltic trading schooner.

Above left: The 9,863-ton Strathconon of P & O enters Sydney Harbour.

Left: The Esso Hibernia joined the great oil fleet in 1970. Her gross tonnage is 126,539 (deadweight 250,262).

Right: Sailing barges in the Thames.

construction of these giants, were the worst affected. Only Brazil, Poland and South Korea reported an increase in orders for tankers. A total of more than forty million tons deadweight (eighteen million gross) was cancelled in that year.

Meanwhile insurers faced enormous losses from tanker catastrophes. The vessels on which pay-outs were to be made included the Greek-flag, Panamanian-owned *Kriti Sun* (61,054 tons) struck by lightning off Singapore in October 1975; the 115,441-ton Norwegian *Berge Istra* (223, 963 tons deadweight) which disappeared south-west of Mindanao in the Philippines on a voyage from the Brazilian port of Tubarao to Tokyo Bay with 188,000 tons of iron ore in December 1975; and the Onassis Group's *Olympic Bravery* (275,000 tons) which fell foul

of the Ushant Rocks at the entrance to the English Channel after she had left the French shipyard at St Nazaire for Norway on her maiden voyage in January 1976. Lloyd's of London officially announced the loss of the *Berge Istra* by sounding the famous Lutine Bell, saved from HMS *Lutine* (formerly *La Lutine*), wrecked near Terschelling, one of the West Frisian islands off the Dutch coast, in 1799 when she was carrying an insured cargo of gold worth £1,400,000.

By the mid-1970s tankers accounted for almost half the total British-registered tonnage. Trading vessels of 500 gross tons and more registered in the United Kingdom numbered altogether nearly 2,000. They represented a little over one-tenth of the 290 million gross tons that make up the commercial fleets of the world.

Voyages of Adventure

ON SUNDAY 9 AUGUST 1573, at sermon time, the thunder of guns in Plymouth Sound startled the worshippers at St Andrew's Church and sent most of them rushing out, untroubled at missing the rest of the discourse. Francis Drake was back from the Spanish Main. 'The news of his return', we are told, 'did so speedily pass over all the church, and surpassed their minds with desire and delight to see him, that very few or none remained with the preacher, all hastening to see the evidence of God's love and blessing towards our gracious Queen and country.'

The evidence was a glittering haul of silver and gold captured from the Spanish mule trains at Nombre de Dios on the Isthmus of Panama. Four years later Drake was off on another raiding expedition. On 15 November 1577, he sailed proudly out of Sutton Pool, with a little fleet of 'ships and barks'. Everyone in Plymouth had heard that he was on his way to Alexandria for currants, but there were some who guessed that sooner or later he would arrive in the Indies. The Spanish knew better; one of their agents in London had reported the 'pirate Drake' was planning to kidnap 'the prince of Scotland'.

The civilized luxuries of Drake's cabin in the flagship *Pelican* were almost weirdly remote from the perils and discomforts, the great tempests and barren shores, that lay ahead. Drake was not looking for currants. On the Panama expedition he had gazed out to the Pacific, like Cortez or Balboa 'silent upon a peak in Darien', from a platform in the branches of a very tall tree; and there, high up in a fair wind, he had asked God 'to give him life and leave to sail once in his life upon that sea'.

He sailed into it in the late summer of 1578 through the straits which Ferdinand Magellan had discovered 58 years before.

Besides holding a service of thanksgiving, he changed the name of his flagship to the *Golden Hind*, at the same time placing on her poop the crest of Sir Christopher Hatton, a *hind trippant or*.

Hatton was the Queen's Captain of the Guard and an important shareholder in the venture. As Thomas Doughty, his representative on the voyage, had been beheaded for behaviour tending to 'contention or mutiny, or some other disorder', the change of name was a shrewd stroke on Drake's part. Whatever Hatton might make of the Doughty affair, he could hardly fail to be pleased that the flagship was now called after the hind on his crest. Off the west coast of Africa Drake had acquired a pinnace and named her the *Christopher*, obviously in honour of Hatton, but he had afterwards let her drift.

He entered the Pacific on 6 September, to find, as he said at the time, that 'Mare Pacificum' would have been better named 'Mare Furiosum'. After 70 leagues of ocean wilderness, the *Golden Hind* and her consorts ran into a gale. On 15 September, at six in the evening, an eclipse of the moon began, and while the sea was darkened the *Marigold* vanished for ever with all on board her. From the *Golden Hind* Francis Fletcher, the chaplain, heard their cries blown towards him from 'the mountains of the sea'. The voyagers called these waters 'the Bay of the Severing of Friends'. Not long afterwards the *Golden Hind* and the *Elizabeth* lost sight of each other. Returning through the Straits of Magellan, Wynter's *Elizabeth* reached England a year before the flagship, but the crews of both ships grieved until they met again. Wynter's voyage scotched for ever the belief that no ship which sailed through the Straits of Magellan could ever sail back again.

Early in 1577 a number of meetings had been held in Mortlake, at the home of Dr John Dee, Fellow of Trinity College, Cambridge, the geographer, mathematician, astrologer and inventor of the British Empire. Dee was convinced that ships could reach Cathay by sailing west-about round North America through the Straits of Anian, once the entrance to those straits had been discovered. Beyond lay the unknown Southland, 'Terra Australis Incognita'; for surely Providence would have placed as much land to the south of the equator as to the north of it?

If the *Golden Hind* had kept her old name, says the author of *The World Encompassed*, she would have been a Pelican in the wilderness. In the fierce storms which swept her down to the uttermost part of land towards the South Pole, Drake saw the hand of Providence. He had proved that the Straits of Magellan did not separate the American continent from a vast landmass to the south. There was no 'Terra Australis' along the southern edge of the world: there was Cape Horn where, 'near in 56 degrees' (the exact longitude is 55° 58' 40") the Atlantic Ocean and the South Sea met 'in a most large and free-scope'.

Having rounded the Horn, Drake drew nearer to a region where Europeans had settled. They were, of course, his mortal enemies the Spaniards. The rest of his voyage along the South American coast is an epic of triumphant plundering. Hearing that El Draco, the Dragon, was off the coast, the governor of Chile took to his bed, where he later died. At Lima the church bells sounded the alarm. In Mexico the Viceroy called the citizens to arms. In Guatemala the bishop offered his cathedral bells for cannon metal.

Deeply laden with treasure, the *Golden Hind* made her way further up the coast, her commander hoping that he might find the North-

Opposite previous page : Lieutenant J.R.L. Williams in the Single-Handed Trans-Atlantic Race of 1968. In 1966 he completed the Round Britain Race.

Below : Using knowledge and inspired speculation, Christian Norgaard of Marin County, California, designed this 'replica' of Francis Drake's Golden Hind, *seen here in the Port of London before setting off for California – Drake's Albion. The 102-foot vessel was built at Appledore in Devon, not very far from Buckland Abbey, the great sailor's home.*

West Passage which Frobisher had sought in vain on the eastern side of the continent. He did not discover it. After weather so cold that the ropes were frozen, they came to latitude 38° 30' and anchored where the 'people of the country' welcomed them with speeches and gifts – bunches of feathers and little baskets of tobacco and begged Drake to be their king, or Hioh. He declined, with embarrassment, and accepted their crown and sceptre in the name of Her Majesty across the ocean. Henceforth Elizabeth of England would be Hioh of Nova Albion. The voyagers remained from 17 June to 25 July.

Whatever bay Drake and his crew had entered, they were on the Pacific coast of North America six years before Grenville arrived at Roanoke Island with the colonists whom Drake afterwards took back to England, 28 before Christopher Newport brought the *Susan Constant*, *Godspeed* and *Discovery* into the Chesapeake, and 41 before the *Mayflower* anchored at Cape Cod.

After setting up a monument, they made straight across the Pacific, spending 68 days at sea with never a glimpse of land. Drake's prayer in Darien had been gloriously answered: he had navigated that mighty sea from side to side. From Java he crossed the Indian Ocean, and on

visitors had helped themselves to so many souvenirs that nothing remained for ourselves but two articles of furniture made from her timbers, a table in the Middle Temple, London and a chair in the Bodleian Library at Oxford.

On one of the islands off Cape Horn, during a lull in the storms, the men of the *Golden Hind* had come upon a plant like the pennywort, or pennyleaf, which grew in Devon. Long afterwards some other sailors from England were reminded of home again and again in unknown seas on the far side of the world. They had anchored in a bay which had oysters 'as good as any which ever came out of Colchester'; they had seen rivers that reminded them of the Thames; and they had had goose pie for Christmas after a gale had blown their ship out to sea.

The vessel which had carried them thousands of miles to unmapped shores had been built for the North of England coal trade. She was the *Endeavour Bark*. We do not know for sure even the primary dimensions, much less the details, of the *Santa Maria*, the *Golden Hind* and the *Mayflower*; much has to be inferred from other knowledge. Captain Cook's *Endeavour*, however, was a Whitby collier, of 366 tons burden, 97.7ft along her lower deck and 81ft along the keel, with a breadth of 29.2ft and a depth in hold of 11.3ft. Such details as her painting and varnishing are known. She was built by Fishburn

15 June 1580 he rounded the Cape of Good Hope: 'This Cape is a most stately thing and the finest Cape we saw in the whole circumference of the earth.'

Months later, in the autumn, some fishermen off Devon were astonished when a West Country voice hailed them from the deck of a ship passing Rame Head: 'Is the Queen alive?' She was indeed; and in the following April she knighted Francis Drake on board the *Golden Hind* at Deptford. The ship – a replica of which, built in Drake's Devon, is now in Nova Albion – was ordered to be preserved for ever. By the middle of the next century she had fallen to pieces, and

of Whitby in 1764 and put into the coal trade as the *Earl of Pembroke*. The Admiralty bought her in 1786 and renamed her the *Endeavour*; adding the work 'Bark' – not to be confused with 'barque' – to distinguish her from an *Endeavour* already in the Navy List.

Describing the qualities needed in a vessel suitable for exploration, Captain Cook himself wrote:

A ship of this kind must not be of a great draught of water, yet of a sufficient burden and capacity to carry a proper quantity of provisions and necessaries for her complement of men, and for the term requisite to perform the voyage. She must also be of a construction that will bear to take the ground, and of a size which, in case of necessity, may be safely and conveniently laid on shore to repair any accidental damage or defect. These properties are not to be found in ships of war of forty guns, nor in frigates, nor in East India Company's ships, nor in large three-decked West India ships, nor indeed in any other but North-country ships such as are built for the coal trade, which are peculiarly adapted for this purpose.

James Cook knew all about Whitby colliers. At eighteen he had gone to sea as an apprentice and served in small vessels touching along the coast between the coal ports and London. In 1768, when he set out as Lieutenant Cook on his first voyage of discovery, he was experienced in coastal and deep-water navigation. He had served under Wolfe and had attracted favourable attention with his survey work in the St Lawrence and on the coast of Newfoundland: sailing directions for Newfoundland waters are still largely based on his observations.

Long before the crew of the *Endeavour* had their goose pie Christmas dinner among the Three Kings Islands in 1770, Abel Janszoon Tasman of the Dutch East India Company had abruptly sailed away from those waters, leaving a great question still unanswered: 'We trust that this is the mainland coast of the unknown Southland?' The question had been asked ever since ancient times. Could an inaccessible part of the earth be inhabited? James Cook was determined to settle the problem for ever. At six o'clock on the morning of 19 April 1770 those on board the *Endeavour* (she had left England with five officers and 88 men) saw land extending from north-east to west.

We continued standing to the westward [Cook wrote] with the wind at south-south-west until eight, at which time we got top-gallant yards across, made all sail, and bore away alongshore north-east for the easternmost land we had in sight, being at this time in the latitude of 37 degrees 58 minutes south, and longitude of 210 degrees 39 minutes west. The southernmost point of land we had in sight, which bore from us west one-quarter south, I judged to be in the latitude of 38 degrees south, and in the longitude of 211 degrees 7 minutes west from the meridian of Greenwich. I have named it Point Hicks, because Lieutenant Hicks was the first who discovered this land.

The first Briton to set foot in New Holland, the land that would be called Australia, was Isaac Smith, a midshipman and a cousin of the commander.

After returning home in 1771, Cook said that another voyage was needed to settle the question of the Great Southland. On his second expedi-

tion, which began in 1772, he had two ships, the *Resolution* and the *Adventure.* The *Endeavour Bark,* after sailing into history, returned to her unromantic duties, but her commander thought so highly of her that he was given two similar vessels. The 462-ton *Resolution* and 336-ton *Adventure* were Whitby colliers, nearly new when the Admiralty bought them. They were carrying a total of thirteen officers and 177 men when they left Plymouth in July. On the first voyage Cook had taken with him, besides the equipment needed for observing the transit of Venus, a pocket watch, the *Nautical Almanac* and Hadley reflecting quadrants and a sextant, two recent inventions. He now had a copy of Harrison's perfected chronometer; both 'watch machines' are still ticking away at the National Maritime Museum.

On his return in 1775, he wrote to a friend at Whitby: 'I was now fully satisfied that there was no Southern Continent.' Hardly less important was his discovery of how scurvy could be prevented by strict attention to diet and cleanliness; the ships themselves were constantly 'cured with fires' or 'smoked with gunpowder mixed with vinegar'. In three years he had not lost a single man from scurvy.

Having satisfied himself that 'Terra Australis' did not exist, the great navigator directed his attention to that other centuries-old puzzle, the existence of the North-West Passage. He chose the *Resolution* again, and left in company with Captain Charles Clerke on board the *Discovery.* She, too, was a Whitby collier, the smallest of the four at just under 300 tons. Unfortunately she was badly fitted out in the royal dockyard at Deptford where incompetence, indifference and corruption reigned. Cook said that the second-hand gear left over from coal carrying always lasted longer in his vessels than the new material from the dockyards.

Altogether the two ships had thirteen officers and 163 men. They carried such a collection of cattle, sheep, horses and goats that Cook described the *Resolution* as resembling Noah's Ark. Her master was William Bligh, later to command a ship called the *Bounty.*

Sailing northwards from the Sandwich Islands, the mariners entered the North Pacific and came to 'the longed-for coast of New Albion'. They had arrived off Drake's shore almost exactly two centuries after the *Golden Hind.* It is strange to reflect that while they were travelling, like Drake, past lonely shores, and meeting only occasional Indians, the American colonists were fighting a war to free themselves from British rule.

The Indians at Nootka Sound proved to be experts at helping themselves. 'Before we left the place,' says Cook, 'hardly a bit of brass was left in the ship.' They departed on 26 April. On 9 August they reached the westernmost point of North America, which they called Cape Prince

of Wales, and to the sea which they entered they gave the name Bering after the Dane from Petersburg who had explored it half a century earlier. The great inlet on the American side they mapped as Norton Sound, in honour of the Speaker of the House of Commons.

Cook had been told to investigate the North American coast as far as 65 degrees and then search for the passage leading towards Hudson Bay, or Baffin Bay between Greenland and America. If he could not complete the exploration in the first season, he was to winter at a convenient place and try again in the summer. In the event, having too little time left, he decided to retire south and winter in the Sandwich Islands. He did not return. 'It is with the

utmost concern,' announced the *London Gazette* in January 1780,

> that we inform the public that the celebrated circumnavigator, Captain Cook, was killed by the inhabitants of a new-discover'd island in the South Seas. The Captain and crew were first treated as deities, but, upon visiting that island, hostilities ensued and the above melancholy scene was the consequence. This account is come from Kamchatka by letters from Captain Clerke and others. But the crews of the ships were in a very good state of health, and all in the most desirable condition. His successful attempts to preserve the healths of his crews are well known, and his discoveries will be an everlasting honour to his country.

The news that the great explorer had been stabbed in Hawaii travelled to London from Siberia, Captain Clerke having sailed back to northern waters and made contact with the Russians at the harbour of St Peter and St Paul (now Petropavlosk). A month after turning south again he died of tuberculosis. Captain John Gore, who served on all Cook's voyages and had been in the Pacific with John Byron (the poet's grandfather) and Samuel Wallis before him, took the ships home by way of China. When they arrived in the Thames they had been away for over four years.

No one could detect an entrance to the North-West Passage, but the attempts to find it added to man's knowledge of his own planet. John Ross and William Edward Parry, for example, made important contributions in 1818 when they explored the Baffin Bay area in the *Isabella* of 385 tons and the *Alexander* of 252. In the following year Parry continued the search in the 375-ton *Hecla*, accompanied by the brig *Griper* of 180 tons. Hecla and Griper Bay was one of his discoveries.

In 1820 Parry set out again. He was to search from the east towards the west, while John Franklin explored from the other direction. The two did not meet. Parry later made a Polar voyage in the *Hecla* and Franklin, after many further adventures, himself became the object of a great search when his ships, the *Erebus* and *Terror*, disappeared on a quest of the Passage in 1845. They anchored near the island of Disco on the west coast of Greenland, and no more was seen of them. Sir James Ross, and then Sir John Richardson, looked for them in vain. The Government offered a reward of £20,000 to which Lady Franklin added £3,000, for news of the party. In the autumn of 1850 fifteen ships were searching.

After years of continuing silence, Sir Leopold McClintock put out in the *Fox*, a steam yacht of 170 tons. Led by various clues, such as a naval button worn by an Eskimo, McClintock discovered a cairn on the north-west coast of King William's Island. A blue ship's paper left by one of Franklin's officers related the fate of the expedition. The vessels had been abandoned on 22 April 1848, after being locked in ice since September 1846, and Sir John Franklin had died on 11 June 1847. Other relics were found, some to be preserved at the United Service Institution in London. While Franklin was credited with 'the priority of discovery' of the North-West Passage, an award of £10,000 for finding it went to Sir Robert McLure and the men who had sailed with him in the *Investigator* on one of the searches for Franklin.

Reading of Franklin's adventures, a boy called Roald Amundsen, born on 16 July 1872 at Borge in south-east Norway, decided to become a Polar explorer. He served as mate with the Belgic Antarctic Expedition of 1897, gained his captain's ticket, studied terrestrial magnetism in Germany, and then left in a 47-ton smack to explore the waters around Norway and Greenland. For a second voyage he acquired the *Gjøa*, a fishing vessel 69ft long and 20.6ft in breadth, with a 7.7ft draught and a 3ft freeboard. She had been built at the Rosendal yard in Hardanger Fjord, Norway, in 1872 and for 28 years had been employed in the herring fishery. Amundsen gave her a thirteen-horsepower two-cylinder engine and had her hull and decks strengthened against ice.

She took him through the North-West Passage.

Left: The Fram *in the ice. After taking Nansen deep into the Arctic, she carried Amundsen to the South Pole – and now enjoys a happy retirement in Oslo, Norway.*

Above: Scott's Discovery. *Since 1937 she has been moored in the Thames at London, off the Victoria Embankment.*

Right: Parry's Fury *and* Hecla *which joined the long search for the North-West Passage.*

triple-expansion engine of 220 indicated horse-power.

In 1896, at the end of amazing journeys by sea and land, he reached home, to be honoured as the man who had been further north than anyone before him. The little *Fram* had not ended her career. After the North-West Passage expedition, Amundsen took her over for a new expedition which he was planning. He had set his heart on being first at the North Pole. In 1909 all was ready for his departure when the world learnt that the Pole had been reached on 6 April by Robert Edwin Peary from Pennsylvania who traced his interest in the North Pole to Nordenskiöld's *Exploration of Greenland*. Leaving the ship *Roosevelt* in the ice, a party of six – Peary, his Negro companion Matthew Henson, and four Eskimos – had completed a sledge journey of 140 miles. From Newfoundland the explorer sent the message which ruined Amundsen's plans: 'Stars and Stripes nailed to the Pole – Peary!'

The Norwegian immediately turned the prow of the *Fram* in the other direction. On 14 December 1911 he arrived at the South Pole, to be followed on 17 January 1912 by Robert Falcon Scott who had made the sea voyage in the *Terra Nova*.

There is a model of the barque-rigged *Terra Nova* at the London Science Museum. She was built as an auxiliary whaler of 744 tons gross, 187ft between perpendiculars and 31ft in breadth. She was built of wood in 1884 for Arctic whaling and her engines developed 140 nominal horse-power. After her Antarctic service she joined the Newfoundland sealing fleet and in September 1943 was lost off South Greenland.

The *Gjøa* and the *Fram* still exist. After Amundsen's voyage through the North-West Passage, the *Gjøa* battled her way to San Francisco through the fierce storm of October 1906. In April the city had been almost destroyed by the earthquake, but the explorers received a tremendous welcome. It was arranged that their

He left with a selected crew on 16 June 1903. Sailing through Coronation Gulf, the voyagers reached the mouth of the Mackenzie River.

Nearly a quarter of a century earlier an American expedition had tried to reach the North Pole by way of the Bering Strait. Its ship, the *Jeannette*, was wrecked in 1881, off the coast of Siberia, and in 1884 articles from the wreck were found on the south-west coast of Greenland. On reading of this discovery in a Norwegian newspaper, Fridtjof Nansen realized that they must have drifted on a floe right across the Polar Sea. 'It immediately occurred to me,' he wrote, 'that here lay the route to the Pole, ready to hand.' On 26 June 1893 he put out from Rækvik with eleven companions in the 400-ton *Fram*, a three-masted schooner which could also use a

ship should stay at the Mare Island naval base until the opening of the Panama Canal, when she would be the first ship through; but a little while afterwards she was bought by the Norwegian colony in San Francisco and presented to the city. She was there for 66 years. In 1971, just before the Amundsen centenary, the Gjøa Foundation asked for her return, and she was sent home on board the Norwegian *Star Billabong* to be restored and placed on permanent display at the National Maritime Museum in Oslo. The *Fram* has a home of her own in the same city: at the end of her active life she was hauled up a specially-constructed slipway and an attractive building was erected around her.

No Polar expedition ship is more famous than Captain Scott's *Discovery*, a Dundee-built wooden vessel of 1,620 tons, 198ft long and 34ft in beam. She took Scott to the Antarctic in 1901 and was away a little over four years. The Hudson's Bay Company acquired her in 1905. She took munitions to Russia in 1915 and performed various other duties. When Shackleton and his party were stranded on Elephant Island, the *Endurance* having been crushed in the ice, she left with a rescue party, only to discover at Port Stanley that the help was not required. She then sailed for Montevideo and loaded grain for France, where she was kept in coastal service, carrying grain to the smaller French ports, until 1920. The rest of her active career was spent on exploration and survey work, in the Falklands area and Antarctica, and by the time of her return to England she had steamed nearly 150,000 nautical miles. In 1936 she was taken over as a memorial to Captain Scott and a training ship for Sea Scouts but her upkeep proved difficult until the Admiralty had her refitted as HMS *Discovery*, flagship to the Admiral Commanding Reserves. She lies in the Thames, not far from the Houses of Parliament and Westminster Abbey.

Exploration in the Pacific did not end when Captain Cook sailed northward. His own work in southern waters was completed by Matthew Flinders. In the sloop *Norfolk*, of 25 tons, Flinders and his Lincolnshire friend George Bass proved that Tasmania was an island by sailing right round it. The Admiralty then sent him off in the *Investigator*, a vessel of the same breed as Captain Cook's, to find out if the eastern part of New Holland was separated from the rest by a big strait. He sailed until his vessel was beyond repair and then left for England to get another. The wreck of the ship in which he was sailing as a passenger led to a series of adventures and to his being imprisoned as a spy when he put in at Mauritius. The French held him for six years. He gave some of his familiar Lincolnshire names to the places he discovered without knowing that one day they would be joined by such names as Flinders Island, Flinders River and

Flinders University. It was he who suggested that New Holland should be known as Australia.

In the great age of Pacific exploration the Dutch, British, Spanish, Portuguese, and French – one of whom, Louis Antoine de Bougainville, has an island called after him as well as the bougainvillea – helped to complete the map of the world. The Dutch were active from an early date. Christopher Newport was at sea with the *Susan Constant*, *Godspeed* and *Discovery* in 1606, and in that same year Willem Janszoon sailed the yacht *Duyfken* out of Bantam to explore the whole of New Guinea. He reached the gulf of Carpentaria, as it would be known, and Cape Turnagain (Cape Keerweer). Ten years afterwards Dirk Hartog, on his way from the Cape of Good Hope to Java in the *De Eendracht*, went ashore on an unknown coast and set up a pole with a plate engraved by one of the sailors: 'On October 25, AD 1616, the ship *Eendracht* arrived here.' In 1696 Willem de Vlamingh, master of the *Geelvinck*, found the plate – it is now in the Rijksmuseum in Amsterdam – and took it with him to Batavia, leaving an inscription of his own. There are almost as many Dutch names in the history of Pacific discovery as there are in the history of art.

Modern exploration is largely concerned with surveying and research in the spirit pioneered by Captain Cook. Two especially notable research voyages were made in the nineteenth century, the first of them by Charles Darwin and Captain Robert Fitzroy in the *Beagle* and the second by Captain George Nares and his companions in the *Challenger*. The giant turtles and iguana lizards in the Galapagos Islands awakened young Darwin to 'that mystery of mysteries – the first appearance of new beings upon this earth'. He was 22 at the time; at 50 he published *The Origin of Species*.

HMS *Beagle* was a ten-gun brig of 242 tons burden, only 100ft long. Officially HMS *Challenger* was described as a steam corvette – she had an engine of rather more than 1,200 horsepower – but for most of the time she depended on wind and canvas. She was a three-masted, square-rigged wooden ship of 2,300 tons dis-

great navigators'. There was a day when he passed through the Torres Strait on a voyage from Sydney to Mauritius, 'commanding very likely the first, and certainly the last, merchant ship that carried a cargo that way'. He came out of the strait – before dusk fell:

Just as a clear sun sank ahead of my ship I took a bearing of a little island for a fresh departure, an insignificant crumb of dark earth, lonely, like an advanced sentinel of that mass of broken land and water, to watch the approaches from the side of Arafura Sea. But to me it was a hallowed spot, for I knew that the *Endeavour* had been hove to off it in the year 1762 for her captain, whose name was James Cook, to go ashore for half an hour. . . .

Left: Darwin's Beagle *at Sydney Harbour in 1841. The future author of* The Descent of Man *and* The Origin of Species *was 22 when his friend J.S. Henslow, Professor of Botany at Cambridge, invited him to join HMS* Beagle *as naturalist on an expedition to South America and the Pacific.*

Below left: Erebus and Terror in a storm *by Beechey. They left England in May 1845 on an ill-fated quest for the North-West Passage.*

placement, about 200ft long overall. Sailing from Portsmouth in 1872, she circumnavigated the world, logging over 68,000 nautical miles on a voyage that lasted 1,000 days.

Endeavour, Resolution, Adventure and *Discovery* – the names of James Cook's ships sum up a great era on the oceans. One word is missing: courage. In the achievement of the discoverers and explorers by sea there is inspiration for us all. Joseph Conrad said that he was never lonely at sea because he had with him 'the company of

Thus the sea has been for me a hallowed ground, thanks to those books of travel and discovery which have peopled it with unforgettable shades of the masters in the calling which, in a humble way, was to be mine, too; men great in their endeavour and in hard-won successes of militant geography; men who went forth each according to his lights and with varied motives, laudable or sinful, but each bearing in his breast a spark of the sacred fire.

Above: A Cautious Landing *by W. Hodges. Captain Cook arrives at Tana, New Hebrides, in 1744.*

Index

ACKNOWLEDGMENTS

The publishers would like to thank the following individuals and organizations for their kind permission to reproduce the photographs in this book:

American Museum in Great Britain (Cooper-Bridgman) 30–31 above; Australian War Memorial 53 above, 58 below right; Stewart Bale Ltd. 74 centre; B.T. Batsford Ltd. 65 right; Bristol City Museum and Art Gallery 34 above left; Camera Press endpapers, 104, (J. Messerschmidt) 54–55, (Theo Van Houts) 101 above; Keeper of the Records of Scotland, Clydebank Collection/B.T. Batsford Ltd. 32, 56 above, 70–71 above; Bill Coward 100–1; Cunard 76–77 above, 80–1 below; Daily Telegraph Colour Library 116, (Anthony Howarth) 58 below left; Esso Petroleum Co. 97 above, 107, 114 below; Mary Evans Picture Library 8–9, 14; Keeper of the Records of Scotland, Fairfield Collection/B.T. Batsford Ltd. 44–45 above, 45 above right, 51 centre, 68–69 below; John R. Freeman & Co. Ltd., 34–5, 96 above left; Guildhall Art Gallery 97 below; Victor Hand 77 left, 78–9; Robert Harding 114–5; Robert Hunt Library 43, 50 below; Imperial War Museum 50–51 below; A. F. Kersting 82; Keystone Press Agency 72–3, 77 right, 81 above, 112–113, 118–19; Lithgow (1969) Ltd./B.T. Batsford Ltd. 96 right; Douglas Lobley 75 centre; Mansell Collection 33 below, 64 above; Merseyside County Museum, Department of Maritime History (Paul Forrester) 85 above, 85 below, 86–7 above, 88–9, 90–1, 92–3; National Maritime Museum 38 above, 44 below right, 98 above, 124–5; NMM/Greenwich Hospital Collection 15; NMM (Cooper-Bridgman) 6, 10–11, 18, 87 below; NMM (Fotomas Index) 98–9; NMM (Michael Holford) 38–9, 48–9 below, 96 below, 120 above, 121 above, 123, 124 centre; NMM/George Rainbird Ltd. 124 above; NMM (John Webb) 19, 42–3, 48 above; Oceanic Containers Ltd. 106 above; P & O 65 left, 76 below, 80–1 above, 81 below, 111 above, 110–111 below, 114 centre, (W. W. Lloyd) 68 above, 69 below; Parker Gallery 45 below; Photri 40, 59, 119, 120–1; Picturepoint case, 1, 2–3, 10, 16–17, 48 below left, 49 above, 101 below, 102–3, 104–5, 122–3; Popperfoto 4–5, 26, 34 below, 50–51 above, 51 above, 56 below, 56–7, 58 above, 62, 68 below, 69 above, 70 below, 74–75 above, 75 above, 75 below, 76 above, 80 below, 84, 86 below, 88 left, 88 below right, 91, 99, 126, 128; Port of London Authority 106 centre, 106 below; Radio Times Hulton Picture Library 64 below, 66 left, 69 centre, 71 below; Franklin D. Roosevelt Library 46–7; Royal Geographical Society 122; The Director, Science Museum, London 12, 13 above, 13 below, 33 above, 44 left, 74 below, (Cooper-Bridgman) 9, 66–7 above, (Paul Forrester) 25, 28–29 above, 29, 30 below, 38 below; Scott's Shipbuilding and Engineering Co. Ltd./B.T. Batsford Ltd. 66 above right; Skyfotos 94; Spectrum 114 above, 118; United Service Club (Cooper Bridgman) 20–21; ZEFA 57 right, 106–7, 108 above and below, 109, 110–111 above, 110 below, 112.

PDO 81-576